CONFESSIONS
OF A TOP
RECUITER

THE NON-NEGOTIABLE SKILLS FOR
MASSIVE NETWORK MARKETING SUCCESS

BY: ROB SPERRY

CONFESSIONS OF A TOP RECRUITER

THE NON-NEGOTIABLE SKILLS FOR MASSIVE NETWORK MARKETING SUCCESS

BY: ROB SPERRY

TGON Publishing

TGON Publishing

CONTENTS

"Great things are done by a series of small things brought together."

— Van Gogh

INTRODUCTION

You may be new to network marketing, be burnt out in networking marketing, or you may be on fire and looking to learn more. Regardless of where you are, I have been there!

Network Marketing is a rollercoaster in all aspects. I still remember getting my butt kicked my 5th month in network marketing. I worked 80 hours a week. Yes, 80 hours a week was dedicated to network marketing. I had already made the huge mistake of quitting my JOB too soon, and now I desperately needed to make network marketing work.

I watched ZERO TV. I read all the personal development books. I didn`t miss any training. I was all in, and committed. Even still, I made less than $400 for the month with all my hard work and sacrifices. There is no way I could feed my family on that paycheck. I was beyond discouraged. I started to blame everyone and everything else for my lack of success.

Deep down, I wasn`t sure if I had what it took to succeed in network marketing. Let`s put this all into perspective. I worked 80 hours a week, so that`s about 320 hours for the month. I averaged just over $1 an hour! What freaked me out even more was thinking about the future. I knew if this pattern continued, I would have to foreclose on my house and file for bankruptcy. It felt like my world was collapsing around me. I felt like I was letting my family down. To make matters worse, the job I had just quit paid me $100,000 a year, and that position was filled immediately after I left, so there was no going back. It was then that I created a simple phrase that helped me overcome the tough times.

"Compensation always catches up to skillset and effort, but it is almost always massively delayed." I kept repeating this quote over and over throughout each day. It helped me shift my focus on the skills instead of the immediate results. This helped me focus more on the process and less on the results, which increased my results.

This book was written to help you shave off decades of headaches and frustration from my personal experience. If you read this book in a few days like many will, it will condense decades in days. Meaning you will discover a new focus and insights from my experiences to reduce your learning curve of doing things the wrong way. I am that guy who did everything wrong numerous times, but through million-dollar mentors and experience, I can and will shed perspective on the skills you must acquire for massive success. Nothing worthwhile is easy, but I promise it will be worth learning. Some skills will be basic, and others will be much more in-depth. Combined, they are the foundational modern-day skills each network marketer needs to grow their business consistently. As always, the only way a book helps is by taking action on what you learn. You can`t become a great pianist by simply reading about it. You can`t become a great golfer by just watching YouTube videos. You can`t become a great network marketer from just reading about it. TAKE ACTION and IMPLEMENT.

When was the last time you evaluated your business, family, or personal life and determined your success?

In the last year in my coaching business, I have helped the largest number of people succeed over any other year. I`m not talking about small wins, either. I am talking about the massive success that we all dream of accomplishing. My coaching clients and mastermind members are the top earners in their network marketing companies. They are creating massive changes and improvements in the world through their influence, philanthropy, and leading by example. They are living with personal success in their marriages, as parents, and in their communities. They are finally starting to create a legacy that will last BEYOND their lifetime.

The most successful people I know have one thing in common: They are consistent in their income-producing activities. Successful people have learned the basic and fundamental skill of consistency. It doesn`t matter if they are building businesses, doing some huge physical accomplishment, or something else. All things come through consistent action.

Over the last five years, I have built a successful coaching business helping people from different network marketing companies become the top earners in their company. I have helped people learn the skills to launch their new businesses and see a vision for the future. I have helped people wanting to get back into the network marketing business after taking time off and found that they can create extra income quickly. All of this was possible because of my consistency.

By consistently developing seven simple skills, you could have a THRIVING, SUCCESSFUL network marketing business. I am obsessed with success and what creates successful people. Over the years of helping hundreds of people create their success, I identified consistent patterns of success. There are seven skills that every single person in network marketing needs to master to be super successful. Here is the best part about the skills, they are simple. People get the wrong perception of network marketing and think it`s too complicated. Successful simply people master the mundane.

A close friend of mine works a 9-5 job. He told me how dissatisfied he is working for a company he doesn`t believe in and selling a product he hates. I said, "you could build a network marketing business if you are unhappy in your corporate job." He laughed and said, "no way! Network marketing is WAY too hard!

After listening to this friend talk on and on about how stressful and complex his job is, it blew me away that he was saying that network marketing was too hard. I told him that network marketing consists of seven simple skills repeated over and over again. They lead to wealth, freedom, and a thriving business.

Successful network marketing businesses are ALL built on these seven skills. Every business model, company, and pay structure follows these seven steps. I am known for saying, "Successful people do the basics better." In this book, I am going to introduce and explain in detail each of the seven steps of network marketing. I wrote this book to serve as a mentor and companion to you and your team as you learn the network marketing skills for success.

Sir Richard Branson is the founder of the Virgin Group, which has more than four hundred companies. He is a total legend and an inspiration for entrepreneurs. When he launched Virgin Atlantic, he got a mentor named Freddie Laker. Richard said, "It`s always good to have a helping hand at the start. I wouldn`t have gotten anywhere in the airline industry without the mentorship of Sir Freddie Laker." Now, I love mentoring young entrepreneurs. American author and businessman Zig Ziglar said: "Many people have gone further than they thought they could because someone else thought they could. Find a mentor."

Not everyone has access to successful people like Freddie Laker, one of Britain`s highest-profile entrepreneurs in the 1960s and 1970s. When asked about his mentorship of Branson, Laker mentioned that he was there to help Branson overcome obstacles and stick to the easy steps of success that too many new entrepreneurs fail to stick with.

When building a network marketing business, it is easy to get away from the basics. Some say you need to invest here, do this trick, etc. Success is built on a robust and firm foundation of the seven basic skills done over and over again. I call these seven basic skills the "foundation for success" for any network marketing business.

I recently spoke at a company event and mentioned that all successful people do the basics better, and I walked everyone through the foundation for success. A woman approached me afterward and thanked me for this training. She had joined her network marketing company, and soon after her sponsor quit. No one else had stepped in to help her figure out how to succeed in her business. No one had told her the HOW of the business. She said she had listened to lots of training on getting her WHY and posting on social media, but no one had walked her through the steps of success in network marketing. When I mentioned that successful people do the basics better, she said, "It was like the light finally turned on! I have been missing the basics."

Sadly, this woman isn`t the only person to have this experience in network marketing. People are introduced to the business, but many do not teach the basics of how to DO it! In order to do the basics better, you have to know what those basics are, which is precisely what we will go over in this book. After you have read this book cover to cover, you will know precisely what the foundational basics of network marketing are and how to execute them repeatedly to create success.

Over the past decade, I have compiled my training, speeches, and notes from my coaching clients and masterminds. As I looked over them and started diving into the basics, these seven basic skills jumped off the pages so clearly to me! I knew I had to write this book so that it could be straightforward for you.

Before we move on, I have to mention one thing. This book is what I call a "companion book." It is not meant to be read alone. You would never dream of only reading one Harry Potter book! The same goes for my books. *The Game of Networking*, *The Game of Conquering*, and *Your Rank Advancement Blueprint* have all been written as companion books to one another. In this book, I will go over strategies and steps for network marketing. In the other books, I cover topics like mindset, networking, and leadership. I promise you, I can TELL you what to do in this book, but if you haven`t gotten your mindset in the right place, it isn`t going to do you any good. I can TELL you how to grow your team, but that team will fall apart if you aren`t growing as a leader. I can TELL you all day where to find people, but if you aren`t learning the skills of networking, you won`t ever put it to good use! So you can see why companion books are so important. You will also want to check out www.sperrybonus.com for more content and great information!

This book consists of seven basic skills. Each section will introduce the step, and then the chapters within the section will give you more specifics about the step and some actionable items you can do. At the end of this book, I have also included a new challenge called "DOING THE BASICS BETTER." This challenge is something that I want every single person reading or listening to this book to commit to. It is a great way to jump into taking action with the seven skills and start to create success quickly. I`d love to follow along with you as you complete this challenge. Tag me on social media using the hashtag #doingthebasicsbetter so I can cheer you on.

There are seven simple skills that you will need to continuously do in your business to create success. Don`t let the simplicity fool you. Some of them will be part of your D.M.O.`s or daily method of operations. Some skills will be used only when the previous skill has been completed, so you may not need to do them daily, so you may create a W.M.O, which is your weekly method of operation. Each skill builds on the other. These skills need to be implemented, crafted, and honed in. As a network marketer, you want these seven skills to become foundational skills that you are continuously improving.

Throughout the book, I will highlight each skill and then give you specifics to work on. So what are the skills? If there is a specific skill that you need to work on immediately, you can jump to that section and begin taking action. Let me introduce the seven simple skills to you.

The seven simple skills every networking marketing professional needs to know:

1. Creating Leads

2. The Art of the Invite

3. Easily Presenting to Anyone

4. The Fortune is in the Follow-ups

5. The QUICK Close

6. Launching a New Team Member

7. Creating Outstanding Culture

SKILL #1 NEVER RUN OUT OF LEADS

"You are out of business if you don't have a prospect."

— Zig Ziglar

Taylor Swift is one of the most iconic singers in the world. I asked one of my daughters if Taylor Swift was the Madonna of their generation, and she said, "Who is Madonna?" Sigh. Taylor grew up singing and performing and is known worldwide for her music. Taylor is known for how much she engages with fans and other celebs on social media. Like many pop stars, Taylor has millions of followers spanning different social media platforms. Taylor takes a bit of a different approach than many other famous people on social media.

Taylor knows the power of connecting and networking to create fans and other people to collaborate with. She uses social media to create connections and build her fan base. In the past, she has randomly commented on fans` pics, has hosted listening parties for her newest albums, and loves to do shoutouts to others. Taylor is also known for connecting with other celebs and working on projects alongside them. Recently she came out with a music video directed by her good friend and actress, Blake Lively. Taylor posted on social media, "I finally got to work with the brilliant, brave, & wickedly funny @blakelively on her directorial debut." When I saw this post, I was reminded of how important networking and posting can be! Blake and Taylor`s fans went wild to see the two of them working side by side on a project. The project instantly became a success. Taylor has been an excellent example of how meeting and connecting with people and fans can continue to create massive success for your business.

You won`t grow a business if you aren`t meeting new people. It`s as simple as that. The first skill to grow a successful network marketing

Your friends and family want to help you but may not want to sign up with you. That`s ok! You can still utilize them for networking and even practicing what to say. But a word of warning, don`t ASSUME that they aren`t interested. Give everyone a chance to say yes!

The best part about family and friends is that you already know each other and don`t have to set a baseline with them. Ensure you stay interested in them while inviting them to look into what you are doing. Start by asking them how things are going or what they have been doing. You can then use one of these scripts for the invite to introduce someone to the products as a customer. In the next section, we will cover the invite and some specific ways to create an invite that doesn`t feel creepy or salesy.

Social Media

"I'm very active on social media and see the huge impact it has on engaging with fans and being able to have a voice."

— Stephen Curry

When Starbucks unveiled its unicorn frappuccino, it hoped it would have an uptick in sales. They had no idea that the unicorn frappuccino would become its own social media sensation. This pink and purple drink became the picture and hashtag that everyone wanted to have. Starbucks was shocked to see how much traffic they quickly started seeing when this drink went viral. With over 200,000 posts about it, it was not long before every store sold out of the picture-perfect drink.

Social media is one of the top revenue-producing tools invented in our lifetime. I am old enough to remember when social media wasn`t a thing. Advertising and getting your company out there consisted of billboards alongside the road, tv commercials, and word of mouth. Nowadays, you can reach billions of people using free apps.

According to numbers I looked up at the time of writing this book:

- Facebook boasts a whopping 2.934 billion daily users

- YouTube has 2.6 billion users

- Instagram has 1.3 billion users

- LinkedIn has 66.8 million users

- Twitter has 76.9 million users

- Snapchat has 493.7 million users

- Tik Tok has 750 million users

That`s an awful lot of social media users, and those numbers change daily. On top of that, these are only a few different social platforms that are being utilized. There are hundreds, if not thousands, more that are out there. At the time I am writing this book, there is quite a buzz around the Metaverse and what that will mean for the next generation. Exciting times to be doing business and finding leads!

Social media marketing campaigns will reach over 50 billion dollars in the next couple of years. Almost every significant brand now includes a social media marketing strategy and influencer campaigns. Small businesses are getting in on social media marketing as well. 95% of small businesses said that their marketing budget would include social media platforms. I include these numbers because I want to stress the importance of using social media. If major brands are using these platforms and investing so heavily in them, it is an excellent way for you to see the value of social media and the power it can have. Companies are heavily invested in strategizing the best plan to make their social media campaigns pay off. While huge companies worldwide invest billions into marketing to get leads, I have great news! You don`t have to. Social media is free, and you can start using it today to create leads by building relationships and expanding your following.

Social media is the new frontier in making money and making an impact. People want to know who they are doing business with. Before I even go into the strategies of using social media to generate leads, I want you to think about how you perceive social media. If you think it`s a waste of time, or you think it`s a big whine-fest with what people post, you will not utilize it. Also, if you are judging yourself and thinking that you don`t have anything interesting to post or are worried about how you look on camera, you will hold yourself back! In my book, *The Game of Conquering*, I talk about fear and where I see people not showing up for themselves. You have to overcome the fear of showing up and creating a life you love to lead! Oh, and I also mentioned that I didn`t make posts about my business or products for the first five years, even after a lot of success. I didn`t post because I had a fear of judgment! Learn from my mistakes.

I encourage you to become a master of at least one of these different online platforms. Start with one and then expand to other social media platforms. It doesn`t matter where they are, but I want you to commit to at least one platform. Make it your job to show up and add value on whatever platforms you choose consistently. To achieve the life you want to live, you are going to have to become more influential. Social media is a great platform to start doing that on. You will also begin to find your voice as you create daily content. Your ability to communicate your message will get better and better. I cringe when I look back at many of the posts from 6 plus years ago, but then I remember that we all start badly. My bad posts weren`t meant to be bad, but now they are an example to others of just starting.

If you scroll on Instagram right now, you will see people post all sorts of things. They post cooking pics, cat videos, and funny memes. These are all great, but often people forget that you are getting free airtime in front of someone. So whether you post cat videos or pictures of your mom's lasagna, I want you to think about what type of value you are adding to the platform and people's lives.

I may be aging myself here, but how many of you remember sitting down and watching tv with actual commercials?! Commercials followed a proven template. They wouldn't just come on and make an offer. They added value first. A commercial for a toy would show kids playing with the toy with their friends. It would show the kids all using the accessories and their imaginations to make the toy that much cooler. It wasn't until the last couple of seconds that we would all learn where to find that toy and maybe how much it was.

People don't stick around if they don't see the value in something. Thanks to social media, our attention spans are getting shorter and shorter. The last thing I heard was that we have three seconds before people decide if they want to see more or keep scrolling. Three seconds isn't that long, but you can add enough value in those three seconds to keep them interested in sticking around for another three seconds or hopefully more.

You can add value in several different ways on social media. Sometimes it's relatability, and sometimes it's humor or even vulnerability. The value our clients see in what we share directly correlates with the amount of attention they give us. The currency of marketing is ATTENTION.

When I first started sharing and going live on Facebook, I struggled to give the correct value and GET the attention that I was seeking from my audience. Looking back, I can see what I was missing! If you want to see some of my first videos, go to "The Game of Networking" Facebook group. You will see for yourself that I was a soft talker.

I didn`t make eye contact with my camera, and my topics were boring even to me! But there was value in getting on and doing those Facebook Lives. Because each time I did them, I got better. Each time I showed up, I learned how to get one more person to stick around for a couple more minutes. I learned how to look at the camera. I learned how to use inflection in my voice during those lives. I showed up very imperfectly, so I could perfect the skill.

So think about social media and think about how you are going to create value for people. This is a way that you`re going to start to increase your market and never run out of leads. Your job isn`t to make sure everyone likes what you are posting. Your job is to share things that you are passionate about. Remember that everyone has opinions and judgments. Their judgments about your posts have nothing to do with you and everything to do with them and their thoughts. Don`t ever let that hold you back from posting!

Trends are constantly changing fast on social media. Whether you create content for lives, reels, posts, or stories, there is one thing that never changes with the algorithms. The algorithm will always reward value!

How do you add value to social media? I want you to pick a couple of your favorite topics that you are most passionate about and start being consistent in posting about these topics. It really can be that simple. Let me share with you what that could look like. Let`s say that your network marketing company is a hair care product. One day you may post hair care tips or maybe even trends in hairstyles. The next day you may post about your favorite activity like hiking. The next day you may post about what an average day is like building a business. Every day`s post can be different, but it all stays on topic with things YOU are passionate about. List all your passions on a piece of paper. Then narrow them down to about five you will talk about weekly. Make one of those five topics connect directly or indirectly to your business/products.

It doesn`t matter what those passions are. What you are doing is attracting the right people to give you their attention. If one thing you are passionate about is politics, I may not give you the time of day, but there are other people out there that will! That`s what you want. You want to start being consistent with your posts about consistent topics. Pick topics that you feel you can be consistent with and are passionate about.

If you are someone who never talks about politics as one of your five main topics but then all of a sudden talks about politics for three to four months, you will abandon your audience. This is only an example. I am not telling you what you should post about, but I am telling you to be consistent on whatever you choose.

You create consistent followers by being consistent yourself. Nowadays, people assume you`re dead if you go silent for a month! HA! Maybe not that extreme, but they may question if you are still in network marketing and if you are still working on your business. It doesn`t matter the online platform you choose to use, but you must stay consistent.

Ben Franklin was a prolific figure. Postmaster, ambassador, founding father, and inventor. Ben had a lot going on, but he knew the key to success. First, he set his intention. He knew he couldn`t focus on everything at once, so he didn`t. Every morning he would ask himself one question, "What shall I do today?" In today`s world, we do much more than one thing a day, but as you look at your schedule, I want you to think about your intention. If you sit down to write a social media post, don`t get sucked into scrolling on your phone for 45 minutes. Set the intention and stick to it.

Now that you know the content you should be posting, let`s talk about how you should post it. Remember the example of the commercial. There is an art to posting content on social media that gets people`s

huge and then fade away quickly. You want to remember that you should adjust to the trends that are taking off and getting attention.

As I write this book, reels and stories are enormous across all platforms. This past month, reels took over as the most-viewed feature on Instagram. Stories and reels on any platform are a great way to draw people in as you go. These features are quick and easy ways for people to get to know you and see what you are all about. Stories are an excellent way for people to get to know you and get a behind-the-scenes look at your life and personality.

One of my clients was very resistant to doing reels. She said, "Rob, I don`t want to dance and do voice overs on silly audio clips. That doesn`t feel great, and I won`t do it!" Good thing for her; that isn`t what all stories and reels are about. You can use them however you want to, but make me a promise that you WILL do them. Figure out what feels best for you and commit to being consistent. I experimented on my social platforms, where I put a picture with some music in the background with a couple of sentences in a post. A couple of minutes later, I put the EXACT same content in a reel. My post got a couple hundred likes and comments. The reel got thousands of engagements on it! I believe that there is value in making posts, stories, and reels. I don`t want you to miss out on adding value to some of your audience because you aren`t willing to try something new!

I have a friend that loves reels on Instagram. It is the ONLY thing he views on Instagram. His wife is a social influencer, and he doesn`t even read her posts! He has purchased several things after watching reels. Don`t leave connections on the table because you are afraid of how you will be perceived or telling yourself you don`t know what to post. You got this.

"You are the average of the five people you spend the most time with."

— Jim Rohn

NETWORKING

A friend of mine saw a lag in his business. He had always known he had a great product, great staff, and service that people needed. But something had changed. It used to be that his business was the only one in the area that provided the service and product that he did. But in recent months, there were two other shops doing the same thing open near him. His staff was starting to get worried as they watched sales start to drop, and some of their best customers did not come back. My friend wasn`t sure what to do, but he knew he needed to figure it out fast.

Upon investigation, he learned that the services were almost identical, and there wasn`t much difference in the product. He knew he had the best staff out there and wasn`t worried that it was a staffing issue. He came to me to see if I could help him find his blind spot. Instantly I was able to figure it out. He wasn`t networking! He had gotten lazy about getting out, creating relationships with people, and maintaining relationships. When I pointed this out to him, he admitted that he had been lacking in connecting and reaching out to others in the past couple of years. He used to be great at it and made it a point to stop into other businesses and people of the community. We sat together and created a networking plan he could start that day. The results were fast! The same day that we met, he had two people that he reconnected with, making appointments to come into the shop and get services done.

Leads run dry when we forget where they are flowing from. Networking leads come from networking with people! Shocking right?! The best way for you to never run out of leads is to continue to be INTERESTED in people. Figure out how to be genuinely excited to get to know others and ask them questions about themselves. Figure out quickly who your audience is. Ask them questions to get to know them better. Learn how to have continued conversations and how to convert those conversations into offers and opportunities.

I learned from an early age how important nurturing relationships is. My parents had a business selling t-shirts and other promotional items. They did a bit of advertising, but their number one lead generation method was word of mouth. It helped that they were selling quality products, but the number one reason people referred others to our family business was my parents. They did an incredible job networking with people and were always interested in others.

I took this lesson and applied it to my business of teaching tennis at age 21. I started via word of mouth with about ten kids who wanted tennis lessons. After each lesson, I would text the parents how their children did. If their child missed a lesson, I would always reach out to see if everything was ok. Every month or so, I would also ask if the parents knew anyone else who may be interested in taking tennis lessons. My tennis program grew to 50 total kids in my first year. We grew to 120 kids in the second year and 280 total kids in the third year. I was able to hire several other tennis coaches to help out, and I was able to build a name for myself in the tennis community. At the age of 24, I landed my first big job, where I started running a tennis club. The average tennis club manager is about 50 years old, and I was 24. In large part, it was all because of my ability to network.

Take a quick second and ask yourself this question, and answer honestly. "Do I care about people?" What was your honest answer? Maybe your answer was, "I care about some people." GREAT! We want to be transparent and honest about where you stand with your thoughts about others. If you honestly answered that you have zero interest in others and hate most people, network marketing probably won`t be for you because network marketing is about people. This business is about caring for and helping other people out with our products and business opportunities. The first book I wrote, The Game of Networking, is dedicated to learning networking skills. It took me SEVEN years to write this book. Some of that had to do with getting over my fears and insecurities, but it also took me so long to write it because I had so much research and concepts to talk about this subject. I am passionate about networking and can tell you that every great thing in my life has happened in one form or another because of networking. In that book, I share three and a half laws of networking that will help anyone become more connected and valued in their circle of influence. The three and a half laws are the law of likeability, the law of credibility, the law of recallability, and the law of profitability. To get a deep dive into networking, get this book! But for now, I want to introduce you to these laws so that you can start to gain the skills to create more connections.

You are surrounded by people all of the time. Even if you are alone in a room, on your phone, you can access people within reach of you through apps and social platforms. Whether people are meeting you in person or online, the three and a half laws of networking will always be in play. You want to get great at every law so that you become someone that people like, think of as credible, recall quickly, and ultimately, someone they trust enough to buy from.

Law one-You must be likable! Becoming likable is a skill that you can develop. Being likable isn`t something that you are either born with or not. You can gain this skill. Being a likable person has HUGE advantages. A study done in the workplace found that people would get promotions over those more qualified for the job because they were likable.

The first place you want to be likable is in your first impressions. When you first meet people, look them in the eyes (if you are in person) and be interested, not interesting. Focus on asking questions you are curious about and want to discuss with others. Make an extra effort to show genuine interest in others. Smile, mention their name, and make them feel important. It is that easy to become likable.

Law two-Be a credible person. So what does being credible even mean? Being credible means **"able to be believed or convincing." When we look deeper into credibility, it comes down to being someone people can trust. People don't believe you if they don't trust you. People won't be convinced by anything if they don't trust you. So when I talk about being a credible person, I want you to think about being trustworthy.**

I was once speaking at a network marketing company retreat. The company brought me in because they struggled to get along. As I met with the leaders individually, they said the same thing about each other, "I don`t trust her." They weren`t finding each other credible sources of information or inspiration. So I had the opportunity to teach and get down to the root of why each of them had lost credibility. It was an honest and raw conversation, but we all came out of it better for being able to talk about it. Six months after the training, every leader who had worked on their credibility with each other and themselves had improved their sales.

So why does being credible matter so much in networking? If people don`t trust you as a reliable source of information, they won`t buy into your product or service opportunity. They also won`t want to introduce you to their network of people because they don`t want to put their credibility on the line for you. The number one thing you can do today to become more credible is to start telling the truth. We all get in the habit of telling white lies or avoiding the truth. Let`s make a pact to stop that right now. We become more credible when people can trust that what we say 100% of the time is accurate.

Law three-Be someone that people can recall. This means that you want to be memorable. You want to stick out. You want to be someone that people think about whenever they think of someone successful, trustworthy, or any other attribute you are striving for. Each of these laws is built on one another. Make sure you are being recalled for the right things! You don`t want to be a person that is remembered for being dishonest or not likable.

A great way to be someone that people remember is to start by introducing yourself in an exciting way. I meet hundreds, if not thousands of people at events where I am asked to speak. The people I remember the most are those who introduce themselves differently than everyone else. Here is an example.

At one of the events I was speaking at, a woman came up to me and said, "Rob Sperry, you don`t know it yet, but you are going to be part of my success story." I was hooked. I had to know more. I asked her her name and how I would be part of her success story. She told me that after she saw me speak, she knew she would hire me as her coach. This woman was spot on with being recallable.

Now, I want to tell you that I had many people mention wanting to hire me or work with me at this event. But not one of them had the recallability that this woman had. As you introduce yourself to someone, think about how you will stand out and be different from others. There isn`t a "one way" to do this either. Every single one of us is unique. Make it your own, but make it memorable.

Law three and a half-The law of profitability isn`t all about money. This law is really about creating a win-win relationship for all parties involved. Too often, people are making connections with others, and they are only thinking about themselves. Maybe some of you have been to networking events where it feels like no one is there to meet anyone, and it feels like a pitch fest. Everyone is there for themselves to pitch their product or service to others. No one likes that!

Before you start a relationship or meet new people, always think about how the conversation, the relationship, or the offer you make is a win-win for both of you. I have several successful friends that make millions of dollars a year. One evening, we discussed how often we get pitched for businesses, investments, products, and ideas. One of my friends asked, "What makes the difference on who you decide to invest your time in?" Every single person said in one form or another, "I give people my interest when the person has thought through how it will be a benefit to me."

As I mentioned before, this is a brief introduction to networking. Check out my book, *The Game of Networking*, to get a more in-depth look into this topic. But for now, I want to answer the number one question I get asked about networking: "Where can I start meeting people and making connections?"

Here is my answer. Start with your interests. Networking shouldn`t be all about business all of the time. You will make better, more authentic connections if you start to network around your interests. I have a friend that loves cars and has built several custom cars. This summer, he went on a road rally down to Southern Utah. This event is where other people bring their epic cars and drive from spot to spot. At each stop, they hang out, find somewhere to eat, and look at each other`s cars.

When my friend returned, he had three different people reach out to him and hire him for jobs. They all had a great time, and not once did anyone pitch anyone else for work or to buy anything from them. This is the way to network! Get to know people. Genuinely care, and take an interest in them. Then, you figure out how you can work together!

Notice that my friend didn`t join the car rally to get to work. He joined because of his love and passion for cars. He was likable, credible, recallable, and he knew how to be profitable in the relationships he made during the car rally. He didn`t pitch during the event and didn`t come off as the creepy sales guy that was there for all the wrong reasons. He used the laws of networking to his benefit.

Suppose you are struggling with where to meet people. You aren`t going to grow a massive business by finding networking events that don`t interest you. You won`t be wildly successful by hitting up every millionaire in your area. You will become successful by finding interests and hobbies that you love and showing up and adding value in those circles. Start with your interests. Join Facebook groups, and find local meet-ups that align with your hobbies or interests. You can even start your own if you have to.

I have coached numerous newbies and leaders to utilize the Facebook Group strategy. Here is what they do. Find a few Facebook groups that have something to do with your hobby or passion. Then go comment on several posts inside the group. This should be easy because it is a group you are passionate about. Then make a post inside the group. As you make a post, try to ask a question inside your post. So, for example, I could find a hiking group. I could make a post about my favorite hikes and then finish by asking what everyone else`s favorite hikes are. This brings your audience into the post and creates massive visibility. Now you can quickly friend request all who comment on your post and shift the conversation to messenger. This is all explained in *The Ultimate Script Book*, but that is a quick recap.

SKILL #1 CHALLENGE

Make connections quickly. I want you to make fifty to one hundred new connections in the next thirty days. Yep, you read that correctly. The connections should be a combination of online and in-person connections. These connections need to be new to you. You can join a new Facebook group, attend an event, or talk to people at the park while watching your kids play.

You also need to RECONNECT with fifty people. These are people that you previously knew that you had lost touch with. This can be relatives, old school friends, people from past jobs, or hobbies that you may not do anymore. Find people you can reach out to and see what they are up to now.

SKILL #2 THE INVITE

> *"If you have the opportunity to do amazing things in your life, I strongly encourage you to invite someone to join you."*
>
> *-Simon Sinek*

Just before Thanksgiving in 2016, a Grandma sent a text inviting her Grandson to Thanksgiving dinner at her house. The only problem was that the invite was sent to the wrong number.

The man on the other end knew that a mistake was made, pointed it out to the woman, and then jokingly asked if he could still come over. The Grandma replied and told him he was welcome to join them for Thanksgiving dinner. The man ended up showing up for dinner, and they created a new friendship. Maybe you heard or saw this story shared with millions on social media. One invite to a wrong number has turned into several shared Thanksgiving dinners and new friendships.

In Paris, a man has opened his home to anyone who would like to come over for an informal Sunday dinner for the past forty years! There could be up to 120 people at the dinner event on Sunday, and an estimated 150,000 people have come over the years. In one interview, the man said, "I was surprised how easy it was to invite people over, and shocked how many have come."

When some people start their network marketing business, they start to complicate the most simple things like the invite. What stands out to you about these two stories? For me, it is how effortless the invite was and what a HUGE impact one single invitation can have in a person`s or multiple people`s lives.

Inviting someone to look at a business opportunity or to try a product doesn`t have to be complex. It doesn`t have to be weighted and tied to your worth or the other person`s thoughts about you. I want to challenge you to stop making invites so complex! Stop making it dramatic and making it mean something that it`s not. Inviting someone to take a look at what you are doing is simple. It can be life-changing for those that decide to look further. It can be that random text that turns into a lifelong friendship. It can be the persistence of showing up consistently every week and watching people start to show up too.

In this next section, I have broken down how to create simple, powerful invites that will get your people interested in saying yes and moving to the next step with you. You will learn how to create connections further, boldly invite people, and use a script that doesn`t sound like a script. Remember, keep it simple! You never know when the next invite is going to create something magical.

"Connection is why we are here; it is what gives purpose and meaning to our lives."

-Brené Brown

CREATE CONNECTION

When Jimmy Fallon first started performing at comedy clubs, he became obsessed with the comedy industry. His skills and connection with the crowd could only get him so far. If he were going to make it in the industry, he would also need to be very intentional with his connections off the stage. Jimmy went to work, ensuring he was using the laws of networking with every person he met. It paid off, and he was connected with an entertainment agent named Randi Siegel. Siegel herself was newish to the industry but had managed to connect and work herself into the SNL crowd and landed clients like David Spade and Adam Sandler.

After Randi watched Jimmy's audition tapes, she called him up, and after she introduced herself, Jimmy said, "Randi Siegel! I know who you are!" Randi was impressed. Jimmy wasn't just a likable guy with some raw talent. He had invested time into knowing the industry and who was behind the scenes.

Randi and Jimmy started working together, and eventually, Jimmy was hired as a cast member of SNL in 1998. Randi reminded Jimmy to stay closely connected and keep learning about the behind-the-scenes people. She told Jimmy that who he knew and how he stayed connected would define his career, and it did.

Jimmy became close with one of the SNL producers, Marci Klein, and she told Jimmy, "After every show, go over to Lorne and thank him for the show." Jimmy took that advice, and after every show, he found Lorne and thanked him again. After a couple of weeks of doing this, Lorne Michaels invited Jimmy to have drinks with him and some celebrities. After that, Jimmy was invited to join Michaels after every show to watch the night's performance. This was a rare friendship that started with making connections.

The connection with Michaels continued to pay off. When *The Tonight Show* was bombing after Leno and O'Brien left, Michaels turned to Jimmy to take over the coveted position. Since he took the position in February of 2014, Fallon has had around four million viewers each night and a higher approval rating than any of his predecessors.

Jimmy Fallon didn't build his career on raw talent. It was built on his ability to make connections and STAY connected with people. It wasn't what he knew, but WHO.

The first tip when creating a connection is to be excited! People love to be around excitement. The energy is magnetic and draws others to you. The first time I approached a good friend about joining me in network marketing, I didn't approach him with enough excitement. I was passive! I said something like, "Hey, I'm doing this thing. It doesn't matter to me if you join or not, but I will do it." YIKES. No surprise that I didn't get him to join that time around. I learned that people don't connect to you, your story, or your offer if you aren't excited.

The second tip is that stories create connections. Once you start networking with people and creating authentic relationships, you want to share your stories and listen to theirs. Stories equal conversations. Conversations convert to sales. When you start sharing stories with others, it will make a huge difference in your business.

When I talk about stories, I am not talking about sharing JUST about how you got started in the industry or about the product you are selling. Sometimes my highest engagement on social media is when I share stories that have nothing to do with coaching or network marketing. I shared the story of teaching my youngest son to do the dishes a while back. There was a video and photos of him suffering in agony over having to contribute and learn to do chores. My messenger BLEW UP! Other parents chimed in to offer support, "Been there! You got this." Some shared helpful tips, "Break it down into tiny tasks and let him succeed at each one before moving to the next." Some even laughed and made fun of it a bit. Every single one of them got a message back from me. This is how we create connections. We think of ways to engage people with stories that are fun and that are relatable to them.

As mentioned, the number one income-producing activity for your DMO is talking to brand new people. This is critical, and your business will suffer if you stop connecting with new people. It is so important, but so many people avoid doing it. If you are talking to brand-new people, you will start generating leads and building a list. As your list grows, your confidence and excitement will and your business will grow, too.

The best way to meet brand new people is to be uniquely you. Let`s face it. Other people in the world are selling the EXACT same product as you. They have a network marketing business with the exact same company as you. So how can you both be successful, attract people to the business, who will buy products from you? You will attract different people because you are both uniquely you.

Your stories are unique to you. Use them. Share them. Let people connect with you through your stories. You don`t need to change or be anyone else to have success. You have to be uniquely you and use stories to interact and bring people into your life that your stories touch.

The last tip I want to share is about making connections. If you find that you are "running out" of connections to make with people, I have to share a hard fact with you. You aren`t running out of connections; you are running out of confidence. There are billions of people on this planet, and we are more connected globally than ever in the history of this planet. If you are telling yourself that there is no one else to connect with, remind yourself that it is a lie. You can never run out of people to talk with. You just need to shift your mindset and build your confidence.

I have taken on coaching my kids tennis teams in addition to writing this book. Watching high school kids play with their intensity and drive is incredible. Most of them have been training in this sport since they could hold a racket. When I decided to help coach, I had to think about my role for the team. Yes, I am a great coach. I have a way of speaking to the players about making adjustments and mindset. But I realized that none of that would matter if I didn`t have connections with them. So before the season started, I laid out a plan of action to create connections with the team. It was intentional and purposeful and made a huge impact. You can be the best person in the world for something, but if you don`t create a connection, no one will ever listen or hear what you have to share. Be intentional with your connections. Spend time thinking about how you want to show up and how you want to create connections. It will end up making a world of difference. Because our family spent the time creating connections with the kids on the tennis team, they are now more willing to listen to my feedback. Create a connection, and the payoff will follow.

"Boldness, be my friend."

— *William Shakespeare*

BOLDLY INVITE

How many twenty four year olds would be bold enough to ask Warren Buffett to dinner? I`m not sure, but there is a story about one woman who did. I read a story about a woman approaching Warren Buffett at a White House reception. Now Warren Buffett is a self-made billionaire. He has invitations to places all over the world. Many people in this woman`s position would have never thought even to make the invite. They would count themselves out before even beginning. But this woman bravely went and made the offer. Here is my favorite part, Warren Buffet said no. Even though he said no, the payoff was still there.

Her bravery and willingness to ask were rewarded. Buffett asked her to join him for drinks and then gave the woman advice and life lessons she will never forget. He told her to ask herself before she went to sleep each night, "Am I smarter? Have I learned something new today?" He also reminded her always to pick up the phone and confront things head-on. Facing fears will always pay off. Finally, he said to be humble, no matter how high you rise. Facing fears will always pay off. This woman`s bravery paid off big time.

So why would I say my favorite part of the story is when Buffett told this woman no? Am I that heartless? Do I find joy in other people failing? Of course not! But I love it when people share when they failed at doing what they set out to do. I think it is an excellent example of being bold. I also love that she was willing to get a no.

Too often, we hold back on being the bolder version of ourselves because we are afraid of what will happen next. Here are the three fears that hold people back the most. First, the fear of rejection. Second is the fear of judgment. Finally, the fear of success. In my book, *The Game of Conquering*, I dive deep into fears and how they impact how we show up in the world. I highly recommend you check that book out to gain better insight into how all different types of fears are holding you back. But for now, let`s take a closer look at these fears.

The fear of rejection is a fear that if someone says no to you, it is saying something about you personally. The woman that asked Warren Buffet to dinner could internalize the "no" from Buffett and think that it was because of who she was, what she was wearing, etc. But you have to remember something. When someone says no to you, it`s honestly about them, not you. Their no is about their own thoughts and boundaries. Maybe they are thinking about you, but that is still on them!

When we can start to become the bolder version of ourselves and start to make bold invites to people, we can STOP taking a "NO" so personally. One of my clients was so scared about being told no. She, thought that meant that the person was rejecting her and not the offer. So I gave her homework to go and make HUGE offers to get no. She hated that assignment but was willing to do it so she could get past this fear. She said, "Just knowing this is my assignment makes it feel a bit better because I am not worried that it will be a no. I know it will be a no!"

A couple of weeks later, we got on our call, and she was excited to report how her assignment had gone. She said she was nervous going into it but started by making bold invites to people she knew loved her. They all said no, and she said I started to see that the word "no" really wasn`t about me. It made a massive impact on her, and she started to get bolder as soon as she dropped the fear of rejection.

The fear of judgment comes up when we are afraid that people will hear our offer and judge us, the offer itself, or any other number of things. I want to let you in on a little secret, every single person judges and is judged. There is not one person that I know of who doesn`t judge others. It is part of our brain`s processes to judge. It is one of the systems that has kept us alive. But, it also gets boring because most of us are rarely in danger of harm or death. So that system that judges to keep us alive also gets involved in other things like what people are wearing, doing, saying, etc. So judgment is happening all of the time, but we have to come back to ourselves and ask, "So what?"

One of my kids came home from school upset because someone at school said they didn`t like their shoes. This child had begged me for these shoes and loved them. I asked them, "What didn`t they like about your shoes?" They said, "they didn`t like the pink laces." Now, this was this child`s favorite part about the shoes. So I reminded them, "Remember how much you like those pink laces? Why does it matter that someone else doesn`t like it." My child stopped and thought about it. "I guess it doesn`t. I do like the pink laces." After that, the entire thing was over. My kid wore those shoes proudly for the rest of the school year without fuss or hesitation.

We hold ourselves back from boldly inviting people because we are afraid of what they will think about the company, the product, or ourselves. We are worried that they will think we are crazy or too pushy. So what? People are constantly creating the experiences that they want to have. Don`t let other people`s judgments hold you back from boldly inviting. Because you never know who is going to say yes! Let them have the option by boldly making the invite to use your product or take a look at the business. The bold version of you doesn`t shy away from offers and invites!

The last fear may sound crazy to some, but the more I coach and interact with people, the more this fear comes up. It is the fear of success. Why would people be afraid of success? Because if they are successful, that would mean they would have to move out of being the person they are now and become a successful person. This means dropping past beliefs, dropping past actions, stepping into the unknown, and maybe even dropping the past version of themselves that they have built up in their mind.

Think back to the woman that invited Warren Buffett to dinner. If he said, "Yes, I would love to come to dinner. I will be there tomorrow evening." Now, all of a sudden, this woman has to think all new thoughts. She has to figure out what to serve, talk about, and several other things. Suddenly, she is the woman who hosts Warren Buffett at dinner. This is an entirely new identity to her.

I see this a lot in network marketing. People are afraid of who they will become when they have success. I met a man at an event I was speaking at. He came up to me after I was speaking and said, "So you`re telling me, to be successful, I can`t party every weekend with my friends?"

I asked him, "What do you think the most successful version of yourself would be doing on the weekends?"

He said, "Definitely not partying with my friends on the weekend. But that would mean I wouldn`t have any friends. That`s the only thing we ever do together."

I asked him if he would give up some of his friendships for success, and that question stumped him. He said he wasn`t sure if he was.

To be successful, you will have to START and STOP doing things. That may include changing friends. So what does this have to do with boldly inviting?

The fear of success can be challenging for some people if they are willing and ready to shift into a different version of themselves. For example, let`s take the man who came to me at this event. How do you think he will invite people to look at his product and company if his friends make fun of him? How motivated do you think he will be if he starts to bring in extra income and his friends give him a hard time for success?

The bold version of yourself has learned how to drop the fears and insecurities that swarm us when we are making invites to people. I want you to think about how you would invite people if you KNEW that you had something unique to offer them. Look at your belief in the product and company you are doing business with. If I believed I had the best product out there to solve teenagers and adults being on their phones 24/7, I would shout it from the rooftops! I would tell everyone I meet that they need to take a look at what I have.

My challenge to you after you read this section, is to get out a pen and paper and write down all of the reasons you want to shout from the rooftops about your company and product. I had one of my clients do this, and she was shocked about how many things she was holding back from offering when she got fearful about what people were thinking about her. As soon as she broke away from those fears, the bold invites started coming, and her sales increased. Remember that if you are genuinely excited about what you offer, it will come across in your invitation.

"Strategy without tactics is the slowest way to victory. Tactics without strategy are the noise before the defeat."

— Sun Tzu

USE THE SCRIPT

When I first started network marketing, I was able to recruit a really good friend into the business. He became a multi-million dollar earner but didn't start that way. My friend decided the best way to launch his network marketing business was to start traveling like crazy. So, the first month he went to several different locations and had a great turnout. Sadly, his closing rate at these locations ended up being very low. He worked eighty hours a week and was very discouraged by the end of the month.

He hadn't come close to hitting the numbers we had set together as his goal, and we couldn't figure out what went wrong. This guy wasn't starting network marketing from scratch. He had an incredible skill set and network to work with from past business ventures. It didn't make sense to either of us what went wrong. We were both very confident that with his success and credibility, everyone would want to work with him.

So he called our mentor and gave him the breakdown of the past month. He told him about his hard work and that he had done everything our mentor had told him.

In a moment of frustration, my friend said to our mentor, "I did everything, and yet the results sucked. What else is it going to take?"

The mentor had sat the entire time silently as my friend spoke. Our mentor said, "I can`t fault your work ethic, but I have to call you out for not following the system."

This blew both my friend and me away. What had he missed?

The mentor said, "Part of our system is third-party validation. Not once this entire month did you set up a time for you and me to talk with any of your prospects."

My friend had felt like the expert. He had felt like he could close anyone and that everyone knew, liked, and trusted him. But he had missed a crucial element. The mentor said, "You tried to use your OWN credibility to leverage your position. You didn`t follow the system and ask for any third-party validation from me."

He had missed a step!

My friend quickly learned his lesson and realized that using the mentor for third-party validation was the missing piece. The following month, he used a third party for everything and completely smashed his goal.

Part of the missing piece was learning how to use a script to get people to some sort of third-party validation. Third-party validation is just hearing another voice. The principle is the same, but the technique varies with each team. Some do group chats, while others do zooms or three-way calls or chats.

To create connections, you must start to see the importance of credibility. Most people are TERRIBLE at creating credibility for mentors and experts. I have listened, watched, and coached hundreds if not thousands of people on what to say to help give credibility quickly to others to help create a fast connection between a prospect and a mentor. Nothing pains me more than seeing a message like this,

"Hey, excited about your interest in this business; my mentor wants to talk to you. They know more than I do."

YIKES! (Sadly, this is a real message that someone wanted me to review and give them feedback on). To validate, give credibility and get people to the next step of the system, you must know what to say and how to say it. It doesn`t matter if it is in person or online. The words are simple and easy if you know what to say. That is why scripts can be so helpful. They tell you exactly what to say and when to say it to help people make connections and move forward.

Connection is made through being genuine with people, and seeing everyone is valuable. Connection is sustained by people`s belief about how valuable you are to their lives and if you are a credible source of information. One of the biggest objections I hear when I mention using scripts is that they think using a script is robotic and won`t help create a connection.

Scripts are a framework! You aren`t going to say every single script precisely how it is written. You have your way of speaking, and you must infuse that into a script. If you shift your mindset around scripts and start seeing them as frameworks, that will help you see how powerful they can be when infused with you and your personality.

My mentor gave my friend a script so that he would know exactly what to say to get people on the phone for a third-party call. My friend adjusted that script to make it sound more like him, and as I mentioned previously, he started to crush his goals and have massive success in his business.

As mentioned earlier, I recently wrote a book with a good friend, Brian Fryer. Like me, Brian is a generic network marketing coach. We have the opportunity to coach, speak, and now be authors together. Our book, *The Ultimate Script Book for Network Marketers: Never wonder what to say again or how to say it* is a collection of ALL of the scripts that Brian and I used when we were in network marketing, plus new ones that we created for our clients. I won`t go over every single script here, but the book will give you a detailed guide on everything scripts. It is the guide to knowing exactly what to say in all situations in network marketing.

Most communication is non-verbal, so even when we tell you what to say, there is also the "how to say it" component that you always need to consider. This goes back to the "making connections" section we just covered. The magic of scripts is more than words. Apply your personality and style to any script you use and watch the magic happen.

When you start to use scripts, remember that you need to constantly be testing them and using your feedback to tweak and fix the parts of a script that aren`t working. If a script isn`t working for you, that doesn`t mean you completely throw it out, adjust small things and see what works for you.

There is a framework to create effective scripts for any concept. Let`s dive into how a simple script will work and why this will help your business. Take making connections with new people, for example. I want to ensure I am likable, credible, and relatable if I meet someone new. By the end of the conversation and connection, my goal is for the person to see the potential of our relationship being profitable (win-win).

The framework to make a connection that will help me will include an intro, a compliment, and a question. That's it! It is simple, but too often, people miss this framework completely! The next time you are around new people, I want you to pay close attention to how people introduce themselves. I was at an event last night, and I heard several people introduce themselves with an intro, a fact about themselves, followed by a story about themselves, and ended with an awkward pause and an exit from the conversation. How engaging is that for the other person?

If we were using that framework in a script for that event, it would look like, "Hey, Britney, I am Rob. I love that Tesla you rolled up in! I just got a Tesla myself. Any tips for a new Tesla owner?"

The script is simple yet so powerful. I use the person's name. I let them know who I am and that I have been paying attention to them even before we met. I ask them a question that helps them feel engaged, and they want to share it with me. The script works, but remember that it is only PART of the connection. If I am having this conversation and staring at my phone or looking around the room, trying to find someone else to talk to, the script isn't going to fix my poor behavior. Scripts can only take you so far!

SKILL #2 CHALLENGE

Come up with your script to invite people to look at the product and another script you will use to invite people to look at the business. You will use both scripts as outlines each time you invite someone new into your business.

SKILL #3 PRESENTING

*"The power for creating a better future is always
contained in the present moment; you create
a good future by creating a good present."*

— *Eckhart Toole*

One of the best presenters of all time is Jim Rohn. Jim was a motivational speaker, author, and entrepreneur. He said, "The more you know, the less you need to say." I highly encourage everyone to go and listen to Jim`s books or snippets of talks he has done that you can find on YouTube. Tony Robbins is who he is today because of Jim`s influence.

At seventeen, Tony Robbins saved enough money to attend a three-hour seminar Jim Rohn hosted. At the time, it cost $35, and Tony had to take his $40/week wages to make that happen. But he was committed to finding the change. In his book, *Money: Master the Game*, Tony said, "It turned out to be one of the most important investments of my life."

"That man, that seminar, that day — what Jim Rohn did was put me back in control of my own future," Robbins writes in his book. "I took [his] message to heart and became obsessed — I would never stop growing, never stop giving, never stop trying to expand my influence or my capacity to give and do good."

You may have heard this story before because Tony Robbins shares it frequently. But have you ever thought of the other side of this story? What do you think Jim Rohn thought when he saw a seventeen-year-old kid walk into the seminar?

It would have been easy for Jim Rohn to give up. He started speaking at high schools and colleges for free and eventually started to get paid for the engagements. But all along the way, Jim focused on becoming the best at his craft. Too often, I see people in network marketing downplaying the power of their presentation. They don`t prepare well enough, they don`t have a message, and they don`t do any follow-up whatsoever.

What would change if you approached every presentation you were giving, whether in person or online, like you had a Tony Robbins in your audience? What would change for you if you believed that your words would change someone`s life? What would you have to believe about yourself in order to be ready for that? That is exactly what we are going to talk about in this section. I guarantee that it can happen to you when you prepare for it, believe it, and take action toward it.

Presenting is a skill you will always want to be working on and crafting. I have been speaking and presenting for most of my working life, and still, to this day, I always do my prep and post work after I have presented. I know how important it is to work on it continually. If you aren`t focused on it, it`s a skill that can fade over time. I once watched someone present who, in his prime, was one of the best presenters in network marketing. When he got up to give his presentation, it was sloppy. It ended up being about him sharing a story without a real connection to the audience. Don`t be that guy.

"It's like I'm there….but not really."

— My son doing online school during the pandemic.

ONLINE

I love the story of how Justin Beiber was discovered. When Justin was twelve years old, he played on the streets of Ontario, and his mom posted videos of him singing on YouTube. A talent manager by the name of Scooter Braun saw the videos and knew Justin had the potential to be a huge star. It all started by posting videos on YouTube.

We live in one of the most incredible times to build a business. We have direct access to billions of people through social platforms, and everyone has a chance to be heard, seen, and discovered.

The online sphere is our opportunity to create content that can be seen by thousands, if not millions, of people. If you ever want a huge laugh, go to Facebook and check out some of the very first videos I ever did. They are so bad; they might just be good! The one mistake I see people (myself included) make a huge mistake in the beginning is not knowing some basic things about presenting yourself online. I don`t want you to make or continue to make the mistakes that so many people do, so in this section, we are going to break down some everyday things to do or not do that will make a massive impact on how you show up online.

I was once asked by one of my clients, "What is the biggest stage in the world that you have presented on." That was easy for me to answer. I told her, "The same one that you have presented, Social media."

Do you see your online presence that way? Do you see how social media and online are the biggest stage in the world? If you haven`t yet, I want you to start to see it that way. We all have this fantastic stage we can get to any time during the day and say whatever we want. So many people are not taking their online presenting seriously enough!

I shared the quote at the beginning of the section because I feel like this is how everyone is presenting online. It`s like they are there, but not really. Let me give you an example. The other day I was on Facebook, and I noticed that my friend had started a live stream. I decided to jump on because at the very same time he was live streaming on Facebook, he was also texting me. I could tell with the live stream that he was there, but not really. He wasn`t engaging with the audience, he wasn`t making excellent eye contact with the camera, and I think he got distracted when I sent him a string of emojis because he stopped mid-sentence to read my text.

Please take your online presenting seriously. Here are some ground rules that you should always follow. First, turn off all phones (unless you are using it as a tool) and other distractions. You don`t need to live stream or record a presentation, look at text messages, do online shopping, or organize your Google Photos while doing a presentation. I see so many people get distracted while presenting online.

Next, engage with your audience! This means from the time you turn your camera on until the time you turn your camera off. Look at the camera lens instead of at the screen. (You would be shocked at what a difference this makes.) Also, don't start interacting after, "A couple more people hop on." There is nothing more infuriating to me than when people have actual people on a presentation and discount them by saying, "Let's wait for the latecomers." If you have people there, start interacting. You can start the presentation in a bit, but start interacting, and don't mention that you are waiting for more people to hop on. If any of you have watched my presentations on Facebook, I always have questions I love to ask people to get them to interact from the moment I jump on. I ask them where they are from, what they plan on doing that day, their favorite vacation spot, etc. It doesn't matter what the question is. The thing that matters is how I start interacting from the beginning.

Next, anytime you are presenting online, you must remember that you have a tiny window to get people interested and engaged enough to stick with you. It doesn't matter if it is a live on social media, webinars, or anything else. You must quickly remind them why they are there and what they will get if they stick around with you. That means you must be clear about why you are showing up online. Before you hit "live video" or start a webinar, be clear about what you want to say. It doesn't matter how long it takes you to say it, but always be aware of how you are including your audience in the presentation.

It can be hard to get feedback in real-time at in-person events, but that doesn't mean you can't "read the room" online. Start to watch the stats and see what is happening. Depending on what platform you are on, you can look and see when people stopped watching or when you didn't have any questions for a while. Go back and ask yourself, "Where did they disengage?" Most of the time, you will find a spot in your presentation that you can tweak and make even better next time.

CONFESSIONS OF A TOP RECRUITER

Finally, remember that you are getting on the biggest stage on the planet! I want to encourage you to get ready for it. We all have different ways of presenting, but ask yourself, "Would I get on stage in front of thousands of people in my pajamas?" If the answer is no, then maybe pause before you hit the "live" button. Maybe you would get on stage with every kid from the carpool in the car screaming and throwing fruit snacks, but maybe not. I want you to be you and be authentic, but just pause and think about how you view yourself and the presentation you are doing before you "jump on for a quick minute."

I am going to share the top secret way I got better at presenting online. Are you ready? The way I got better at presenting online was just doing it. Earth shattering right? I realized that the best way to get better was on the job training, so I started to make offers to people to do small trainings online to their teams, I started to do lives in my facebook group, and I eventually started doing LIVE videos. I committed to doing two lives a week.

I wish I could tell you that engagement was epic, but it wasn`t! In the beginning I was only getting two to three comments on my LIVE videos. That`s because the content was THAT bad! If you go back and look at them, they really were that bad. Make the commitment to yourself and realize that it won`t be amazing in the beginning and that`s ok. You have to get the experience. Even if your audience isn`t listening, you are learning how to find your voice.

Stephen Covey wrote a book about the eighth habit; which is finding your voice. When you are committed and consistent, you will find your voice faster! You will start to learn what to say and how to say it in a way that starts to convert. Always remember, that it`s not going to be perfect, so you may as well start right now and find your voice.

In-Person Events

"The best way to predict the future is to create it."

— Abraham Lincoln

It doesn`t matter if you are presenting or attending an event; events change lives! I have watched it time and time again. I invest a lot of time, energy, and focus of my own business into creating mastermind events because they are so powerful. There is something electric that happens when we come together in one space. When I host events for seven and eight-figure earners, the energy in the room is fantastic, and I can instantly see how much growth and development the people there are getting. Speaking and attending events is essential because where our energy goes, energy flows. So if you are presenting at an in-person event, you will want to ensure your energy is going towards that event.

Since I host so many events, I have the opportunity to invite and watch many different kinds of people present. I have had professional athletes, entrepreneurs, tv stars, etc., come and speak at my events. When presenting, it doesn`t matter who you are or your accolades. You can become a phenomenal speaker. Several years back, I invited someone I looked up to come and speak at my event. I paid this person to come and pour into my group for the allotted time. I was so disappointed when they showed up. It was clear they had done ZERO research into who they were coming to speak to. When they got up on stage, this person spent the entire time talking about themselves with no tangible takeaways or connection to the audience. It was terrible! I was mortified. As soon as this person was done speaking, they jumped off the stage and left without saying anything to me or anyone else at the event. It was such a great learning lesson for me. Just because someone is famous doesn`t mean that they can present at all!

Being a good presenter can be taught. It is a learned skill that I believe every single person should learn. If you have read my past books, you know how shy and introverted I was growing up. I refused to speak at my church when they asked me to because I was terrified to get up in front of people.

At some point in our lives, we will be asked to speak or present something. It may be in our businesses, church, or school groups. You never know, but I believe presenting at in-person or online events is crucial to success. So let`s break down how to ensure every in-person or online event is successful.

First, prepare. Don`t do what that famous person at my event did, and come without knowing who or what you are presenting. Do some research. Ask yourself who will be there, and think about why they would be showing up at this event. Maybe you are presenting a product at a girl`s night out. Great! Think about who will be there and why they would want to come. How do you want to incorporate your product into that fun evening, and how do you want to present it?

If it were me, I would make sure the night was fun. I would think about having things set up and a fun area to take selfies and pics with friends. As I was presenting, I kept it light and fun and always returned to self-care and experiences with friends. This wouldn`t be the time to pull out a twenty-slide PowerPoint with graphs. Know who you are presenting to, and think through the type of presentation that will be best for them.

Think about your timing. An excellent presentation can go wrong if the timing is off. I had several speakers lined up to speak at an event and told all of them that they had about 45 minutes to speak. One of the speakers went WAY over. Their presentation was great until it went long! The attendees started losing interest and were ready to get up and stretch and use the bathroom. It also meant that the next speaker`s time was cut down significantly. At the end of the event, the feedback I heard from several people was that they wanted to hear more from the second speaker and felt like it just wasn`t enough time. So whenever you are presenting, be aware of the time for the people attending and other speakers presenting with you.

I have an acronym that I share with every client that is getting ready to present. It is NENO. It stands for No Event, No Offer, meaning that every presentation and event should end with an offer. You have missed a massive opportunity if you get up and present and don`t make an offer. Always come ready to make an offer during the presentation. The offer can be to take a closer look, get a sample, get on a consult, etc. It doesn`t matter, but there better be an offer! On that same note, you don`t want to overwhelm the people there with too many offers. I once listened to a 30-minute presentation that had sixteen offers in it! Psychologically our brain doesn`t like to process and pick which of those offers to do first. It feels overwhelming, so most of the time, we do nothing. When you are presenting, stick to one main offer throughout the presentation.

One of my favorite questions when preparing for a presentation is, "How does this relate to the audience?" you have probably heard the saying, "facts tell, stories sell," and it is true. Still, you must ensure that the story relates to the people you are presenting. I could tell a tennis story to a very broad group of people because I know how to tie the tennis story back to them. But I would lose the audience`s attention if I just started telling a story about this one match in high school and didn`t tie it back to anything. Before you present and share stories, make sure you are connecting it all back to the audience.

I often get asked what the difference is between speaking to a small intimate group and a large group that fills a conference room. In a small intimate group, you can look everyone in the eyes, read body language and see what resonates with the people in the room. The main difference is where your energy needs to go.

In larger crowds, that gets more difficult. Your energy has to be higher so you can project to the back of the room. You must use the whole stage, so everyone feels included in your presentation. You may only see the first couple of rows, which may be all you get. So you have to get good at reading the room when you can only see a few.

It doesn't matter if there are two hundred or two thousand people that you are presenting to. The concepts I have shared in this section will help you have a successful presentation every time, no matter the number of people. Remember, where energy goes, energy flows.

SKILL #3 CHALLENGE

Host two events online or offline in the next thirty days. This event can invite people to look at your product or a general networking get-together. Be creative! Events aim to work on your inviting and presenting skills.

SKILL #4 THE FOLLOW-UP

*"Follow up and follow through until
the task is completed;
the prize is won."*

— *Brian Tracy*

Think back to what you were doing in eighth grade. I know for me, I was hanging out with friends, annoying my siblings, and trying to get out of my jobs at home. For several kids, the eighth grade is the start of being recruited for prominent colleges like Alabama. College football recruiters and coaches now see the power of follow-up and making connections younger and faster. Some of the country's top recruiters and coaches have started recruiting eighth graders to their teams. One unnamed head coach said, "if you want the best, you have to find them early and consistently follow up with them and their family." Nick Saban was courting a young potential recruit, and his Dad said, "Nick treats us like royalty. They treat my son like a five-star recruit even though they don't know what the next four years of high school may look like for him."

Before starting network marketing, I was approached ten or eleven times about network marketing companies. One of those last times, I was approached by a friend named Brett. I was interested in what he shared, so I let him pitch his offer and business opportunity. I loved what he said about the company, the vision, and the income potential. I was interested, but I didn't want to act like I was too interested.

I acted lukewarm, told him I would think about it, and asked him to follow up with me later. Then, nothing. He never followed up! I still can't believe it. Had he followed up with me, I know I would have said yes. All I needed was one more follow-up. One more check-in. One more "I know we can do this together!" All I needed was one more conversation because I had already decided that if he followed up, this was the chance I was willing to take.

He did end up being successful in network marketing for years and then got into something else. Years later, we ran into each other, and I told him the follow-up story and how I was primed and ready to go if he would have followed up. He sat quietly and said, "If I had

followed up with you, I know I would still be in network marketing."
We both commented that it was a good learning lesson for us. You
never really know where people are at in their life and what they
will say. It is always worth it to follow up. Think about it this way. If
you don`t follow up, you indirectly show your lack of confidence in
your business. Until someone tells you "no," your job is to follow up
because you don`t know what they are thinking. You may be able to
help them through confidence issues, answer questions for them, or
show them how easy it is to get started. In this next section, we will
break down how to create a follow-up system so that you can find the
balance between being persistent and not overbearing, overwhelming,
or overdoing your follow-ups.

"The fortune is in the follow-up"

— Every single leader
in network marketing.

CREATE THE SYSTEM

Over the years, I have heard several reasons people don`t follow up. If you have been in network marketing for more than a couple of months, I want you to think about what excuses you use not to follow up. This isn`t to beat yourself up and judge yourself. This is about being aware of your habits so that we can create a new system around them. The biggest reason people don`t follow up is that they don`t have a system to follow. There was once a study on how successful people will be based on the consistency of tasks. In the study, they had two different groups. The first group was given a list of things to do. They were told they could do them any time of day, but they couldn`t write them down or do them in order throughout the study. The second group of people was given the same list of tasks, and they were told that they had to create a system, a time of day, and a task list that they would look at every day. I am sure you can already guess what the outcome was. The second group was able to accomplish the majority of the tasks and stayed the most consistent. The most interesting thing about the first group was how many people gave up after a couple of weeks into the study. The researchers said that without a system in place, most people were overwhelmed, confused, and gave up.

As you think about your business, there will be several places where you will need to create a system for follow-up. Following up isn't just about getting new clients. Following up happens with your business builders, product users, new clients, etc. You must create follow-up systems that work for you in these different areas.

As you read or listen to this, I can imagine some of you getting overwhelmed. So let's break this down together. Get out a pen and paper or use your phone, and I want you to think about where you interact with others in your business. This will include making connections, making offers and invites, hosting events, signing someone up, etc. Take a couple of minutes and write them all down. Now that you have that list, I want you to go back to write at the top of the page, "Where is the follow-up?" This will help you remember that the ultimate goal of this exercise is to figure out what needs to be followed up on and how you want to do it.

Next, go through the paper and write down each area's what and the how. An example of this might look like, "Invited to online presentation" WHAT? Send zoom link info and remind me about the presentation. HOW? Via messenger two hrs before the event. Some of you may be stuck in the WHAT to say when you are following up and sending out messages or phone calls to people.

You have likely heard the phrase, "The fortune is in the follow-up," but what does it mean?" So many people are doing what I call the "pitch and disappear" approach. Don't be that person! Remember, no script, no system, and no person will be successful without follow-up.

Everyone asks, "How soon should I follow up?" A good rule of thumb is if someone is directly messaging you back, you should check it and respond within 24 hours. The principle is that people change their minds quickly. If they have said yes to the opportunity, and you wait three days, they have already moved on with their lives and may have forgotten the yes already. Not to mention, their excitement has likely dwindled.

One rule of thumb that has always helped me stay consistent with my follow-ups is the BAMFAM acronym. It stands for "Book A Meeting From A Meeting." Essentially this means that before you end a conversation with anyone about anything to do with the business, you should have your next meeting, event or time to connect scheduled with each other. It could be a follow-up call, check-in on messenger, or meeting on Zoom. It doesn`t matter what it is, but don`t get caught without the subsequent follow-up and check-in being scheduled before you leave your last conversation.

Every single interaction will lead to a follow-up. Let`s say that someone wants to buy a product from you. There will need to be a follow-up! You will have to send a product link, answer questions, etc. There is not ONE SINGLE interaction that doesn`t have a follow-up that goes along with it. Even the person that is a "No" will get a follow-up. The timing of the follow-up matters, and we want to be clear that you will need to set up your follow-up system. I asked Coach Fryer to share his follow-up system that led to his and his client`s success in their businesses. This system is key to tracking and remembering where you are in your follow-up process with every prospect and time.

In our script book, Coach Fryer and I talk about the power of follow-up and how important it is to your business to create a follow-up system. Coach Fryer also shared his system for follow-up, which I want to share here. It is the 1-3-7 follow-up formula that thousands of network marketers have used worldwide. It's increased their overall conversion rate by 200% and has saved them time knowing exactly when to follow up and what to say. To get the entire system WITH scripts, check out *The Ultimate Script Book*.

When Coach Fryer started network marketing, he was crazy busy! He was not only trying to build a business but also coaching high-level baseball athletes. As a former professional baseball player, he was always in high demand! He found it hard to remember when and how long to follow up with people in his network marketing business. That is when he created the 1-3-7 formula. This cut out his guesswork with follow-ups and made it easy to follow. Here is the formula and details about how to use it.

1-Day Follow-Up:

- Mention previous conversation

- Don't assume the worst; give them the benefit of the doubt (maybe they just got busy or sidetracked)

- "Hey _____, hope you're having a great day! I'd love to help answer any more questions you may have about _____ (insert problem discussed). How else can I best help?" :)

3-Day Follow-Up:

- No mention of the previous conversation

- View as 'touching point.'

- "Thought I would stop by real quick ____(insert name) and say that I hope you are having a great day/week! Anything fun planned for the weekend?" :)

7-Day Follow-Up:

- Time to create URGENCY

- Insert FOMO

- Come in with a strong offer.

That`s it! That is one way to create a system. Now I want you to go back to the list you made at the beginning of this section. Now is a great time to get even more detailed with the 1,3,7 system and figure out precisely what you want to say and how to say it using this system. In the next section, we will talk more specifically about staying consistent with your systems and why consistency is key to any success in network marketing.

"Success isn't about greatness;
it's about consistency.
Consistent hard work leads to success."

— Dwayne Johnson

CONSISTENCY WITH YOUR SYSTEM

Simon Sinek is a world-renowned author and speaker and has written some of my favorite books, including *Leaders Eat Last* and *Start with Why*. In one of his talks, he spoke about how consistency will always beat intensity when going after more significant goals. Simon said, "We like intensity. We like things that can be fixed fast." Simon then talks about how consistency is key to success with whatever we are doing. When we can stay consistent over a long period of time, we are bound to succeed.

In *Good to Great*, Jim Collins says: "From the outside, they look like dramatic, almost revolutionary breakthroughs. But from the inside, they *feel* completely different, more like an organic development process." Because of the perception, we chase "the single defining action, the grand program, the one killer innovation, the miracle moment that would allow [us] to skip the difficult build-up stage and jump right to breakthrough."

Network marketing can get a bad rap from people talking about instant success and making boatloads of money overnight. Anyone in this industry knows that what is true is that there is great potential that can be sustained and built upon IF we stay consistent with our simple, actionable items like our DMOs (daily method of operation) or WMOs (weekly method of operation).

So what do your DMOs look like? Where are you committed to staying consistent over time? How are you going to be successful in this business?

A client once asked me if I could have a thirty-minute coaching call with a new builder they had brought on. My client was stuck trying to mentor this guy because he kept saying that the business model they were following was broken and wasn`t sustainable. I got on a call with this gentleman and quickly realized where the issue was. This guy was about fast hard action, but he didn`t have any consistency behind his work ethic and efforts. As he told me how the system was broken, I asked him, "What are the simple daily actions you are taking that are moving you forward?" He said, "I don`t need the small stuff! I need the big BOOM in my business! I want the explosive action that gets me results." If I were to use a different example, it was like he was trying to lose weight overnight instead of sticking to a food and workout plan consistently over time.

It`s easy to believe that we can go with the big BOOM plan and get results, but those results won`t last. I have watched people try and sustain their businesses one big thing after the other, which never works in the long run. YES, we want to have times we push in the business, we call these blitzes, but we want to ensure that we are creating a DMO plan that is working for us and helping us stay consistent over the long run.

I want to share with you my personal DMOs that I did every single day while I was building in network marketing. I still follow most of them today, but it has shifted a bit now that I am a coach.

Daily Method of Operation (The amount for each category depends on the speed you DECIDE to go in your business)

- 1 New Post or FB Live

- 5 New Reach Outs (A reach out is a non-business message. It could be a new contact, or it could be an old friend. It is simply staying connected with others)

- 1 New ASK (Directly asking someone to look at your products or business)

- 5 New Friend Adds (Adding five new friends on social media)

- 1 Follow-Up

- At least ten pages of personal development

Now some of you will create a WMO for specific goals instead of a DMO. For example, I work with many top leaders who prefer setting a weekly goal for new invites. You want your WMOs and DMOs to be simple. Don`t try to overcomplicate the system because you will never follow a complicated system. I once had a client come to me distressed by her DMO system. She wanted me to look it over and see where she could make it easier. I told her I was happy to look at the system and send it over. She hesitated and said, "Well, it`s not that easy because if THIS happens, then I follow system number one. If this other thing happens, then I follow system number two." On and on, it went on until she had shared seven different DMO systems with me! Stop complicating your daily methods of operations. This system is not an "If this, then this" type of system. You are willing to complete your daily method of operations tasks, even on your off days.

Here are some rules I follow that have helped me succeed with my DMOs. Rule #1 Have a consistent routine. We all know how tempting it is only to work when we are "in the mood." Almost every successful person I know has an established routine.

Try this: For each of your goals, write down one thing that must happen for you to achieve those goals. Now go to your calendar and block out time for that task. Every day it is planned; you show up and do what you planned. Whether you feel like it or not.

Rule #2 Work in compartments. Work will continually expand to the space it is given. I have watched it time and time again. Benjamin Franklin, who I think was one of the most efficient people ever to live, was a huge advocate of working under time constraints. He built them into his daily schedule. Every task he did had a beginning and an end to it. You would never find him lazily typing away or losing track of time. He was the master of time and used it to the best of his ability. You can do the same by working in compartments. This means you stick to the schedule you made in rule #1 and don`t move out of the compartment until the time is up.

Rule #3 You must define your priorities. Success is determined by the decisions we make on a day-to-day basis. Most decisions we make are not thought through with our priorities in mind. We may think that our priority is our business, but when we look at your choices, it tells an entirely different story.

To make better decisions, you must create clear priorities in your life. What are your values? What do you want to create in your life? What would you want to focus on if I could guarantee results a year from now? When you know what you care about, you can start to make better decisions about where you are spending time.

Rule #4 Track and reflect on your progress. Establishing DMOs and WMOs requires consistency. You won`t know how you are doing if you aren`t willing to track. That`s one reason that Benjamin Franklin built himself a simple tracker. He wanted to know how he was doing and be able to make decisions based on fact and not emotion alone.

If you don`t do what you say you will and have been tracking that, it is hard to tell yourself a made-up story about how nothing is working for you. You can pull up and see that it isn`t working; YOU aren`t working. Make it simple for yourself, and start tracking your DMOs. Each day, record whether you showed up or not for each task.

As you are tracking and ask yourself each night, "what good have I done today?" This will help you reflect on what is going well and give yourself credit where credit is due. Once a week, I want you to ask yourself three questions, "What did I accomplish?" "What lessons did I learn?" "How did I evolve and grow for next week?" If you can be honest with yourself and not beat yourself up for anything you are discovering about yourself, I promise you will start seeing results. This is how we can start to guarantee progress.

I remember one day, I wasn`t feeling well, and I could tell I was coming down with something. I looked over my DMOs and knew that they were something I could do even when I wasn`t feeling the best. I showed up, did my DMO, and then put myself to bed. The entire time I was sick, I was able to complete my DMOs. You know yourself best, so I`m not saying that it is best to work when you are sick, but I am saying that you want to make your DMOs so simple that you CAN do them if you are sick.

Just like Simon Sinek has said, "Consistency will win." I have stayed consistent with my diet and exercise plan for my adult life. It has always been important to me. I knew that I could create a simple, actionable plan that had no exceptions, and I could create a life that would have me living in optimal health. My plan isn`t perfect. It`s not sexy, but it has created the success that I would not trade for anything. Figure out a system and stay consistent.

*"When the solution is simple,
God is answering."*

— Albert Einstein

FOLLOW UP
WITH SOLUTIONS

Depending on your age, you may have grown up watching Mr. Rogers on the PBS network. Mr. Rogers was known for taking complex, challenging problems and breaking them down simply for kids to figure out. He tackled problems like facing anxiety, divorce, and losing a loved one. I loved listening to Mr. Roger`s straightforward approach to problems. One of my favorite quotes from Mr. Rogers is, "We all have different gifts, so we all have different ways of telling the world who we are." That also goes for coming up with solutions to problems.

One thing that most people forget about following up is that we are here to help people with problems. When we are following up with people, we aren`t just following up for our benefit. We are following up so that we can help people solve problems that they are facing.

All people everywhere have problems. Scroll on Facebook for two minutes, and you probably stumble on people complaining about something. It could be a broken car, the algorithm not working in their favor, or they are struggling with their finances. Sometimes we forget that the best way to follow up with people is to offer solutions to problems that they are having.

When someone buys a product from you, they will want to get their money's worth out of the product. To do that, you will have to help them learn the product's best uses. They probably bought the product because of a pain point they are having in their lives, so you will want to ensure that you help them get their money's worth while also solving the pain point with them. How do you do that? You create a system for new users of your product that will help support and educate them about what they have purchased.

I have a friend who doesn't have a network marketing company, but she has bought several different products from several companies. We were over at her house, and I saw the unused products and asked her, "What's up? Why haven't you used any of these products?" She told me she loves buying products but rarely gets anyone who helps her learn about the uses and benefits of the products she has just bought. What a loss for those people! They were willing to follow up to the point of the sale, and then they went MIA.

You will also need to find or create a system to help people learn new skills to succeed in this business. Once a new person signs up, how do you teach them to learn the business? How do your systems help them stay committed? How can you continue to support the results they are after? The answer to all of this is a system. I love it when people have a system that can walk the newest person through how to make their investment or get into the business quickly. Remember that quick wins help people stick around longer.

The last system that will help solve problems is the system of investment. We are continuously investing in ourselves because our minds, body, and soul are the only ones we get! We want to make sure that we are making wise investments in ourselves. One big pain point I see in this industry is when people have used all of the systems and training in their own company and are looking to seek more learning, experience, and a new skill set. Often people don`t know where to turn to get the support they need. That is one reason I became a coach. I wanted to be a generic coach that was supportive and respectful of all network marketing companies so I could help people looking for more support and skill level to help support and uplift the business they are growing.

People will always have problems. We can either watch them wallow in their problems, or we can help create systems that will uplift and solve problems for people. You don`t have to get tied up in the drama of people`s problems; you must simply find the system and solution and offer it to them.

Anytime you are following up, I want you to start thinking about it as an opportunity to offer solutions to people`s problems. Your follow-up system is based on being solution based. You want to be known as the person who has solutions. You want to have people know that you are always willing to help. Start seeing your follow-up as an opportunity to help people solve problems.

SKILL #4 CHALLENGE

Create a follow-up system for yourself that will make the most sense. It can be the 1,3, 7 system or something else. Create something that sets yourself up for success and follow it for the next fourteen days with all your interactions, invites, presentations, and offers.

SKILL #5 THE CLOSE

"The one thing in life you can control is your effort."

— Mark Cuban

Mark Cuban is best known as the owner of the NBA team, the Dallas Mavericks, and is also one of the stars of the TV show *Shark Tank*. Mark is a Billionaire who first started his journey into entrepreneurship at a very young age.

When Mark was twelve, he focused on getting his first pair of Nike shoes. He had seen the shoes and asked his dad to buy them for him. His dad had said no and had told Mark that when he had his job, he could buy whatever he wanted with his own money. That got Mark motivated to go out and get a job. He realized that if he wanted something, he had to go out and work for it. With the help of one of his Dad`s friends, Mark started selling garbage bags door to door.

His dad`s friend charged Mark three dollars, and Mark turned around and sold them for six dollars. Mark said he instantly fell in love with the business and doing deals. We all know his drive, but how did he get so good at closing deals when he was only twelve? Mark said, "The key to selling is connecting with people and serving them. You are not trying to convince them of anything. You are trying to show them how you will make their lives easier. It`s a win-win for everybody."

What a great reminder to all of us! When we think about selling products or inviting people to look at the business, we must consider your mindset. Do you believe that you are bothering people? Do you believe it is a BIG ask to pitch to your friends? Remember that this business and your offers are a win-win for everybody.

The close can be the scariest part of network marketing for people. I remember when I started, I would have people interested, and they would follow up with me, but when it came time to close, I would get so nervous. My biggest fear was that I would become part of the NFL, the "no friends league", if I tried to close them and they said no or didn`t like my product or company once they signed up. I was terrified that I would also lose friends if I tried to close them hard on an offer I had made. I`ve never severed a friendship or relationship in this business because I`ve always treated others respectfully. I`ve always treated others where I make it about them, not about me. You`re not going to be one of those sleazy salespeople that makes everything about them because they want to hit their sales goals.

Another thing that terrifies people is not knowing what to say, whether they say yes or no. In this next skill, I will teach you exactly what to say. You have to remember that the goal is progress. It doesn`t matter where you are right now in your network marketing business and how you feel about the close. There is always room for improvement. This entire business is a journey. You`re not going to learn it overnight. Pick something new that you can learn, and then track your progress. The ultimate goal is to become the person that can help others launch into the beginning of this business. To do that, you will need to learn how to become a master of the close.

If you are brand new to network marketing, I can`t stress enough the power of three-way calls/chats, especially when you are learning to close. I still use three-way calls/chats to this day! But the power of the three-way call/chat is that you are learning in real time with real people how to listen, work through objections, and close. Anytime you use a three-way call/chat, ensure you are taking notes and learning!

There are two questions that every single person asks themselves when they are looking at starting a network marketing business. The questions are, "Can I do what you're doing?" AND "Is it worth it?" You will want to write these down and remember them because as you look at closing new business partners, these are the questions that they will ask you OR be thinking to themselves as they look into this business.

Tony Robbins says that we make every decision based on how it is linked to pain and pleasure. Everyone will base their decisions on how it is linked to pain or pleasure. Remember that when listening to them share their stories or pain points about their lives. As we get into this next section, I will teach you how to gauge people's interest levels, overcome objections, find solutions to their problems, and close prospects quicker.

Qualify what they want

"So tell me what you want, what you really really want."

— *Spice Girls*

To close any deal, we have to be able to see where the prospect's interest level is. It is very unlikely that you are going to close someone who is a one on a scale of one to ten. But if you have someone who is an eight, you can likely close them and get them signed up or order products. One thing to mention about the interest scale, their interest can swing very quickly back and forth. You may be talking to someone with an eight on the interest scale, and then the next day, they sound like a two when you close them. Don't let that discourage you! If you see this happen, remember that questions are always the answer. You need to ask questions to understand what changed for them overnight. Maybe they were excited and told some family members who dislike network marketing. Maybe they were afraid they would not be able to cut it and they let their negative self-talk get to them. You will never know unless you ask the questions.

To qualify people and see where they are at on the interest scale
and overcome any objections they may have, you must get good at
managing your emotions. I once had a very emotional client whenever
someone would swing back and forth on the interest scale. She would
take it so personally when she felt they were at eight or nine, and
then they started to hesitate. When she would ask what happened, it
came off as accusatory and judgemental. She lost people right before
the close, and it was easy to see why. Don`t take fluctuations on the
interest scale personally. Don`t see objection and hesitation as a
personal thing about you. You have to understand that you are talking
to people who are different from you. They don`t have the same
thoughts and feelings that you do. So be open, curious, and neutral as
you are qualifying where they are at. See objections as the prospect
giving you the playbook for what they need to be answered to say yes.

Qualify what they want, and don`t have a plan that only serves you.
In network marketing, most companies have two main groups of
people: product users and distributors. Before you close someone, you
must know what group the person in front of you is most interested
in. Don`t lose product users because you are so focused on finding
distributors. I know from decades of experience that product users DO
become distributors, but some of them need to start with the product
first. You can`t make someone sprint if they want to walk. I always
say, "Walk with the walkers, jog with the joggers, and sprint with the
sprinters." This is all about knowing what they want and meeting
where they are. Our goal in this business is to mirror people.

I remember when I first started in network marketing, I was all about
my OWN goals. I was too heavily focused on what I wanted, and I
missed some great product users and people that could have grown
with my business eventually, but I tried to sign them up as distributors
based on my goals. Setting your own goals is great, but you want to
make it about helping people. Help them decide so that you can help

them solve their problems, and you will find that you can easily reach your goals.

When I see someone with an interest level above five in the product or the business, I always ask one question. This question helps you see where they are and can help set the stage for the rest of the close. The question is, "What intrigues you most about this business or product?" As the person starts talking, you will share with them all the legitimate reasons why you believe this is an excellent fit for them. No fluffy compliments here! People can see right through it. You want to ensure you are building their belief while sharing your own. You want to find what interests them and see what they are thinking. This question helps get you into their brain. This is a huge step that most don`t do.

So why does this make such an impact? Because if I am trying to qualify where they are at and what they want, I can completely miss the boat if I try to paint my own vision for the future. One of my clients told me about a time he forgot to ask this question. He went on and on about how great the business was and how making extra income could allow the prospect to pay for a trip to Disneyland. The prospect scrunched their face in disgust and said, "I hate Disneyland." The prospect interest level went down on the scale! To impact individuals, you must first know enough about them and cater the conversation to them. Find their needs and fill them.

Qualifying what people want means that you can ask curious questions about them and listen. It means that once you hear what they want, you qualify it with them by saying something like, "so what I`m hearing you say is that if you had extra cash every single month, you would take that money and pay off your car?" Qualifying what people want is a simple tool, but people often don`t use it. With social media and feeling like you "know" people based on what they post, people stop interacting and having real-life conversations. Let`s get back to more of that! Every single person that starts in this industry has a dream. Whether it`s the dream of retirement, Disneyland, or paying off their car, it doesn`t matter. You have to know what their dream is so you can speak to it. You are selling a dream. Be careful that you don`t try to sell them on your dream because that won`t line up with them. It`s not about you. Determine what intrigues them most about the business, product, or service, and keep asking questions.

Uncertainties-find them and solve them

"We can't solve problems by using the same kind of thinking we used when we created them."

— Albert Einstein

Once we go through the questions about what people want, we want to find where their biggest concerns are. I always let people know that everyone has fear. Fear isn`t bad; it`s normal and natural. A lot of the time, fear is good because it means you are thinking about things. I get excited when people come to me and tell me they are interested in doing this business but have some concerns or fear! That means they are thinking deeply about what it would look like to do this business. I always mention this to people; it empowers them to go deeper into figuring out what is compelling about the business or product. At this point, I am not going in-depth about the product or comp plan. I keep it simple, and I continue to ask questions like, "what are you most concerned about?" and "what fear is coming up for you?" "Why does this particular thing concern you?" "What other concerns or fears are coming up?"

Rather than trying to avoid their objections and fears, I meet those head-on with a willingness to work through together. We get so afraid to hear people`s objections. Why is that? As I mentioned previously, it is because we are afraid of personal rejection and what we make it mean about us. Stop taking everything so personally. Things only have meaning if we give them meaning. It doesn`t do you or your business any good when you think it`s all about you. We are all self-interested, but in this business, we have to put our interest in ourselves to the side so that we can sit and listen to people and be entirely focused on them. Let me give you a vivid example to help you deal with objections. Imagine a waitress asking if you wanted coffee with your breakfast. Now imagine you simply saying no thanks. Would that waitress be highly offended? No! That waitress probably thinks this person doesn`t want coffee right now, and that`s no big deal. Be the waitress or waiter with your business when someone says no.

I remember this one time my son`s friend got hurt at our house. He scraped his knee and was bleeding. At that moment, I wasn`t worried about what this kid or his parents would think about me. I was wholly focused on helping this boy get out of pain. I knew we would have to clean up the knee and get a bandaid. I also knew he was pretty worked up, and I wanted to help him calm down and know that we were there to help. Notice that when someone is in pain like this, most of us don`t question what to do. We step in and do it. Be willing to step in and help people out. Why does that change when we see people in pain around things like money? Just because we can`t see blood or tears doesn`t mean that people are in just as much pain as this boy at our home.

As you step into help, there will be objections, concerns, or fears. That isn`t a problem. That is what you are here for. As I was helping clean up this boy`s knee, he had big objections! He didn`t want his knee to be touched, he didn`t want the small rocks cleaned out, and he hated the color of the bandaid I had grabbed. None of those were problems. I calmly worked through each objection with this kid, and in a couple of minutes, he was back outside with a cleaned knee and a popsicle.

When people are uncertain, work through that with them. Here are some uncertainties I have heard about when people are starting network marketing:

Uncertainty: "I don`t think I have the time."

Answer: "I will teach you how to do this business at your pace, and we will do it together. Some weeks you won`t work, and some weeks will be full-time. It`s your decision what this business looks like for you. I love working with busy people because I have found that they have a lot more success. After all, they value their time more."

Uncertainty: "I don`t know anything about this type of business or product."

Answer: "We have tools and resources to help you where you will learn all about how to do this business and learn more about the product. I will be with you through the whole process, walking alongside you. I`m going to hold your hand in this business. I`m going to help you; it`s going to be scary, but it`s well worth it."

Uncertainty: "I don`t think I have the money to invest in this business right now."

Answer: "I understand that it is hard right now. I suggest you write down your top ways to find the money. I know it`s not easy, but if you see the value and potential, I promise you that you will find the money. It could be borrowing money from somebody, taking out a loan, selling something you have, or dipping into savings. If you genuinely want this, you will find the money."

I`m not saying it`s easy. Everybody finds money no matter what if the value is there. I don`t know how long it will take you, but I promise you will find the money, and I will do everything I can to help you.

With every single uncertainty, there is a solution. I have not seen one uncertainty, obstacle, or fear that cannot be overcome. But you have to hold that belief yourself. You have to know that you offer solutions that can change people`s lives if they do the work. In all my years in network marketing, I haven`t met one person who told me they couldn`t find a way to do the business it if they wanted to make it happen. These people usually have tremendous success because without sacrifice, there is no commitment. People that make a sacrifice to do this business have more commitment to make this business work.

After you offer solutions, the last thing to do is empower people. Empower them with information and the ability to choose what they want to do. As much as we want people to say yes to all of our offers, they always have to be the ones to decide and make that choice. They may choose to say no. That`s ok. Never belittle or get frustrated with where people are at. Remember that even a no is an opportunity to follow-up. Be kind. Respect people`s decisions. I can`t tell you the number of times I got a no at first, but because I was kind to everyone when their circumstances changed, they came and sought me out to do business with me.

Down the Rabbit Hole

"Start by doing what's necessary, then what's possible; and suddenly you are doing the impossible."

— Saint Francis of Assisi

I have heard people describe starting a network marketing company as a whirlwind. Starting anything new can be overwhelming! My favorite way someone has ever described starting their network marketing company was when one of my clients was telling her story, and she said, "It was like I was Alice in Wonderland and I had taken the leap down into the rabbit hole." That can feel true for so many people. Remember the Alice in Wonderland scene when she falls down the rabbit hole? She doesn't know if she is up, down, or sideways. Alice keeps seeing things in the rabbit hole that make no sense to her, but people that know the story start to see objects and things from the wonderland.

When people start in network marketing, it can feel this way. When you sign up your newest person, remember that it can feel like a lot to them, and to you without a system in place. Your job is to make it simple. Start to give them some foundation so that they can feel secure. I often notice that we sign people up to start the business or even use our product, telling them how simple it is. As soon as they sign up, we throw everything at them! This isn't the best way to start your newest person out. Remember that our job with everyone is to help them solve a problem and get the results. I have taught tennis to people at every single level. I can help the newest person learn to love the game and maybe even hit a ball. I know the exact objective for the first lesson and don't stray away from that lesson.

So your newest person has said yes. Amazing! You now have two objectives that can work together. The first is to help this person get success quickly. The second is to start laying foundational work to help them feel empowered, not overwhelmed.

Let's talk first about quick success.

Think back to what this person's pain points were. How will you give them a simple system to follow that they can do daily? It doesn't matter what you are helping them achieve; I know that if you can start people out with daily accountability, they will see success faster.

As you think about accountability, the first thing you need to solve for them is the best way to get a hold of them and where they can interact with you. You may be new to this industry with zero to a few people who have signed up. If this is you, you may want to give people your cell phone number or email that they can use. If you have a bigger team, maybe you will set up a Facebook group, messenger, Voxer, etc., for people to use.

The ONE THING you must remember is that you have to reply. I don`t care what system you use. Please don`t ghost people. I was at dinner the other night and heard a table beside us talking. They were discussing the most annoying things that they had to deal with. One person mentioned reaching out to businesses and never hearing back. Please don`t be this person. It doesn`t take a lot to reply to people. That being said, I also want to encourage you to set up a system you will use. I had one woman set up a Facebook group and messenger system so that her team could get in contact with her. About a month in, she came to a coaching call and was so upset because her team was mad at her for not replying and being MIA in the group and on messenger. When I asked her about it, she said, "I`m not replying because I never use Facebook or messenger. I just set it up there because I thought that is where everyone would want to be." Big fail! You have to set up a system that you are willing to check in and reply to people.

Once you have set up communication, keep it simple. What is the next step they need to take? That`s it. Share the next step. Some of you may be questioning this, but there is a method behind this. I don`t like to give people ALL the steps because it overwhelms them, so they don`t have a reason to check in with me. They could do the steps alone. I want accountability and a chance to check in with my newest people. So giving them one step at a time helps not to overwhelm them, but it also shows me who is doing the steps and coming back. I always tell them, "Do this one thing, and then Voxer me when it`s done and I will tell you the next thing to do."

Your upline or company may have a system in place that they use, and that`s great. Use it. There is no sense in your reinventing the wheel in the beginning. Make sure it is simple and if you have to, break it down even more for your newest people. Breaking it down to a step-by-step process helps people get more wins faster.

So when I talk about wins and successes, there are a couple of things we will define as a win. I define win and success as two different things. A win is any action taken. In network marketing, people are often only praised for the next rank hit or trip won. Don`t be that type of leader. One of my all-time favorite leaders I work with celebrates people taking action. She has set up prizes and has created a culture around celebrating actions, not just success.

Success is when a person has succeeded at something. For example, if I ask someone to get one new person scheduled for a three-way call/chat, there may be several wins and one success. The wins could be making a list of people to call, calling the people, and making offers. Success is when someone gets someone to say yes to a three-way call/chat and gets it scheduled.

Celebrate all along the way. This helps people feel seen, supported, and recognized. I have co-written several books, and in each, we discuss the importance of celebrating people along the way. So many of the book`s co-authors share what works for their teams regarding the celebration. Make sure to check them out if you need ideas on how to celebrate your team members.

The next thing I mentioned is your objective for the newest person would be to help them get a solid foundation in what they are doing. One of the best ways to help people succeed is through education and action. I combine the two because I see too many people get stuck in the education cycle. They learn and learn without ever taking action.

You want to teach people from the beginning that they will get educated, so they can swiftly take action.

Take a product user, for example. Most companies are going to have some education behind using their product. It doesn`t matter if you sell clothes, skincare, or anything else. You will have your newest customers educate themselves and then take action.

One of the best systems I use to build a solid foundation is to create an education and action plan. Think about the newest person and ask yourself, "What do they need to know right now?" That answer is education. Next, you want to ask yourself, "how are they going to learn it?" Is it a video from the company? Is it time spent with you? Is it reading a brochure or watching YouTube? Once you know this, the next question is, "What are they going to do about it?" This answer is the action that they will be taking. Write it down and write down what the win will be after that action is taken.

These tools are not earth-shattering. They are effective and will help the newest person get exactly what they are looking for every time. One thing you will need to solve for yourself is where this education, action, and accountability is taking place. We touched on this briefly, but I can`t stress enough getting a framework in place. Most of the time, your upline or company will have something, but not always. This is one of the things that I help clients get into place. I have even helped companies audit their systems to ensure they have the most impactful onboarding systems. It doesn`t matter if you have a system to use or if you have to create your own. Get something in place that makes it easier for your newest person to get quick success and build a solid foundation.

SKILL #5 CHALLENGE

Find the objections before they even happen and learn to address them. Make a list of objections you have had or have heard other people in your company talk about. How can you address those objections before they arise when you are working on the close? Next, develop a script that helps you boldly invite people to purchase a product or sign up with the business. Finally, follow skill #6 when someone says yes and is ready to go.

SKILL #6 LAUNCH YOUR TEAM MEMBERS

"If everyone is moving forward together,
then success takes care of itself."

— Henry Ford

Jeff Bezos, the founder, and CEO of Amazon, started his working career at McDonald`s. He said the ketchup dispenser that hung on the wall once got stuck open and ended up dumping almost four gallons of ketchup on the floor. The most interesting thing about any celebrity working at McDonald`s is the training they must undergo to succeed at the golden arches. McDonald`s keeps it simple with a four-step training program. They are trained to Prepare, Present, Try-out, and Follow-up.

So why does one of the world`s most successful fast food chains keep it simple while training their newest employees? They know the power of keeping it simple. They work through the four steps in their program repeatedly until the recruit can pass off each step. They take their employees through the four-step process with each system that needs to be learned to work. For example, during the preparation step, the employee would learn how to get their station ready. In the present step, the employee would learn how to work the station. In the try out step, they would then work the station with coaching from the trainer. Finally, in the follow-up step, the employee gets feedback on what they did well and where they can improve.

When you are training your newest recruit, I love to follow a system I call "24/72 and beyond" This system helps train and support people through the most crucial times when they first sign up to start the business. So let`s walk through this system together. Let`s say that someone has signed up to start a network marketing business. They are excited and a bit nervous. You will help them get all signed up, congratulate them, and ensure you have information to stay in contact with them. They are on a high from the conversation with you and the possibilities of what their future can hold.

There is usually a lot of mind drama in the first 24 hours after people sign up for network marketing. Then real life sets in. They tell their spouse or friend they just signed up to start a network marketing business and are met with an unenthusiastic response. If people are left to their thoughts for too long, they may give up before even getting into their back office. It is crucial to stay in contact with your newest person. Remember how we talked about always scheduling your next appointment/meeting before you are done with your last one? This is the perfect example of that. When signing the newest person up, you will want to schedule a time to talk with them twenty-four hours later. They may have questions come up, or they may be in their head and start to doubt themselves. The twenty-four hour follow up is about reminding them what you talked about and answering any questions. This is also a great time to give them their next step. Before the twenty-four-hour follow-up conversation ends, you will set up your next check-in with them within seventy-two hours maximum.

Once the appointment is set, you will use the assumptive gratitude follow-up text to remind them of your appointment or the specific task they were given. Tasks could be checking out a post in a Facebook group or even checking out a video. You do the following. Send them a text thanking them for taking the time to (insert whatever they committed to). This works because you are being genuine. Aren`t you grateful they are taking the time? Didn`t they already commit? We don`t want to doubt their commitment, so we thank them. Do this, and I promise you the follow-up success will be improved.

Three days, or seventy-two hours, gives people enough time to complete the first task you have given them. Maybe they had completed it before then and moved on to step two or three. Great! Keep that three-day appointment. You want to be able to have a scheduled time to answer questions and see how they are settling into this new business. Within three days, you will notice patterns and what type of person you are working with. I mentioned walkers, joggers, and sprinters previously. I have found that in a three-day window, you can start to see if people are walkers, joggers, or sprinters. There is nothing wrong with the pace people go, but it will help you know how much support you will offer. I find that 24/72 can be high-pressure times for people. They are committed but still unsure what they have signed up for. They may start to have business owners` remorse or even let the opinions of others get in their way. The 24/72 are times when high support and holding belief are crucial.

I call this system 24/72 and beyond because, after seventy two hours, it will look different for different groups of people. You will see how the person is doing and put them into one of the three categories, walker, jogger, or sprinter. Each group is going to need something different. You may find that your sprinters may need a daily call first to keep the momentum going. They may also be the type of person needing very little accountability and more training. You may find that your walkers do great in Facebook training and need weekly accountability and the next step to take. Be sure to decide what YOU are willing to do with each group.

I once had a walker that wanted daily check-ins and "chats." I knew I didn`t have time for that every day, but I had difficulty saying no. My mentor reminded me that my vision was to be a leader to thousands of people. He said, "Are you going to have time for chats with thousands of people daily?" Heck no! Even just the thought of that much phone time made me queasy. It was easy after that to set up boundaries and systems around my time and energy.

The "beyond" of this system is all about you and your energy. You have to clarify what you are willing to do with your time for your team and new recruits. Visualize you have a team of one hundred people. How are you going to help support a team and new recruits? One thing I want to mention here; in the beginning, you may have a lot of time to train and support. That`s great if that`s how you want to spend your time. But remember that we want your support and training to be duplicatable and make sense for how much effort and the time your newest person is putting in. If you put three hours a week into them and they put thirty minutes in, you are setting yourself up for disappointment. We never want to end up being resentful of the energy and time people put into their businesses. Our job as their upline and mentor is to support and not overdo it.

Deliver the Dream

> *"All our dreams can come true;*
> *if we have the courage to pursue them."*
>
> — *Walt Disney*

Can you imagine writing yourself a check for ten million dollars and then believing that someday you could make that ten million dollars a reality? That is exactly what Jim Carrey did. Jim is a famous comedian who starred in several huge movies in my childhood. It is estimated that Jim is worth 180 million dollars. Jim Carrey says he has always believed in the power of manifestation through visualization. He said, "As far as I can tell, it`s just about letting the universe know what you want and then working towards it while letting go of how it comes to pass."

To help your newest team members launch successfully, you must know what they want. You have to be great at figuring out what they want to be involved in and learn how to help them create and deliver that.

One of my clients dreamed of creating a non-profit organization that would focus on creating a better community, neighborhood, and culture in the neighborhood she grew up in. She had come from what she called "the rough part of town," When she started seeing success in her business and life, people from the old neighborhood would call her and ask her for money. She wouldn`t give them money but always offered them the opportunity to learn how to do what she did. Very few people took her up on that offer. It broke her heart to see a community perpetuating the struggling story. She had the vision to break that cycle and create a community that would thrive and uplift from the inside.

Anytime she mentioned what she wanted to do to anyone else, she would always be met with other people`s opinions. They would tell her that it would never work or would be a waste of money and resources. Other people judged her and said, "Who do you think you are? Thinking you are all high and mighty now that you have money." She hid that dream and didn`t think about it again until we talked about it in a coaching session.

My client said that when we were coaching about making any wild dream happen, it was like this one dream shot right out. She wanted it. She knew she wanted it, and for the first time in a long time, she allowed herself to want it again.

Our job is to be the dream keepers. We help people realize what it is that they genuinely want in life. We help them see the possibility in their life and that they can genuinely have whatever they want if they work hard. To be a great leader, you must never mis-judge someone else's dream. I believe every single person has desires given to them for a reason. I have never wanted to be a fashion icon. Shocking right?! But I know someone that does. She spends time learning about textiles, patterns, fashion trends, etc. Her passion for fashion shows. I believe that is a desire given to her to help her find her calling in life. If we ever start judging other people's pure desires, I believe we are going against something that has been given to them by God. I say pure desires because our desires can get off track. Some people desire pornography, drugs, etc. These are the false desires that can distract us from our true purpose. Your role is to see the best in people. See them for what they can become.

We help deliver the dream by helping people return to their pure desires. We can help people find their calling in life. I see so many people living out of alignment with their desires and purpose because they are living paycheck to paycheck. It is hard to dream and have pure desires when we stay up at night worrying about how to keep the lights on in the house and food on the table.

Our job is to help hold people's vision of their future when it is challenging to hold it for themselves. We can do this by asking the right questions and then keeping a file of what the person says so that you can help remind them and paint the vision when it gets hard for them to remember why they are doing this.

For each person I enrolled, and even now, I keep a file on each of them for my current clients. I have written down their goals, what they desire most in their life, their vision for their future, what drives them when they are pumped, and what gets them out of bed when they don`t feel like it. I want to encourage you to do the same. Start a file for every single person that you sign up. Update it as they accomplish things. Update it as their wants and desires change. Check in at least twice a year and ask them the same questions. Hold that vision and belief for them when things get complicated. A great place to create that file is through contact mapping. www.contactmapping.com. This website manages all your contacts and details about them.

One of my clients has been coaching with me for a long time. The other day I reminded her of the first time we coached together, and she told me about her dream. She started crying and said, "I look back and think about how small that dream was, but I remember how big it felt at the time." This woman has made millions, owns several homes, and has created a life she could have never dreamed of when we started coaching together. I knew it was possible for her, so I believed in her even when she didn`t know what it looked like. I held belief for her even when her belief about herself was small. Believe in people doing extraordinary things. Believe that everyone has potential for magic in their life. Believe that with God, all things are possible. Then turn around and show people how to do the same thing.

"The way to get started is to quit talking and begin doing."

— Walt Disney

TAPROOTING

In March 1848, there were roughly 157,000 people in the California territory; 150,000 Native Americans, 6,500 of Spanish or Mexican descent known as Californios, and fewer than 800 non-native Americans. Just twenty months later, following the massive influx of settlers, the non-native population had soared to more than 100,000. The people just kept coming.

By the mid-1850s, there were more than 300,000 new arrivals. One in every ninety people in the United States lived in California. These people (and all of this money) helped fast-track California to statehood. In 1850, just two years after the U.S. government had purchased the land, California became the 31st state in the Union.

As the boom continued, more and more men got out of the gold-hunting business and began to open businesses catering to newly-arrived prospectors. Some of America's greatest industrialists got their start in the Gold Rush. Two, in particular, would use their taprooting skills to become some of the most successful entrepreneurs of the time. Henry Wells and William Fargo moved west to open an office in San Francisco, an enterprise that soon grew to become one of America`s premier banking institutions. They saw a need and jumped at the chance to open a bank in California. As soon as they opened, they trained their staff to always end each interaction with "tell your friends" OR "do you know any other people looking for a reliable bank?"

At the time, almost all business was coming from word-of-mouth referrals, but few people had the skill of knowing HOW to ask for referrals correctly.

Taprooting is the skill of getting into someone`s circle of influence. At the beginning of most people`s businesses, they don`t have a level of influence over a huge majority of people. That`s ok! You don`t need that to start, but you do need the skill of taprooting. Your goal is to sponsor an entire circle of influence. The average person knows 2,000 or more people. Taprooting is a skill that everyone can learn, but it will take time and a lot of trial and error to develop. This means the first thing to taprooting is going out and getting a lot of practice. This is a skill that you will be using all of the time. It is also a skill that will be ever developing. Taprooting takes time for your credibility to catch up, but once you have credibility and skill, you will see how fast your business can grow.

When I started in network marketing, I quickly became the number one recruiter in my company. Years later, I shifted to a large company that wanted me to help them create a rebrand. They asked me if I would come over as a consultant first to create it and then become a distributor to launch it properly. I quickly went to work, listing hundreds of people I could reach out to. I thought maybe if I spent twenty hours reaching out to potential prospects, I could speak with at least fifty people a day. The thought of it exhausted me! I wanted to get sales quickly, but I didn`t want to have to speak to fifty people a day to do it. I was willing to do whatever I needed but wondered if I could use those taprooting skills.

I went through everything I had learned from my mentors on taprooting. I also went through and reflected on everything I learned through taprooting. I recruited one person in the first week and made over $200,000 in sales! That is the power of taprooting.

Instead of going crazy trying to find people, I recruited a high-caliber person and asked them, "Can you get me in front of the very best person that you think is right for this business?" They said yes, and the person they got me in front of signed up. I did this over and over again. I had no time to go out and reach out to those hundreds of people, but I could ask the person I had just recruited to get me in front of their circle of influence. This is the skill of taprooting.

Many of you think, "That sounds great, but how did you get them to put you in front of their best person, and what if that person would have said no?"

Great question! I learned through trial and error that most people are scared that you will say the wrong thing to offend their friends.

I learned to let my new sign-up know that I would not hard sell any of their friends and family but would simply show them the information to help them make an educated decision. Also, please note that I already had massive success, so I could leverage that. When you are on your way to success, you will leverage other people`s credibility to help bridge the gap of lack of credibility. Regardless of if my sign-up prospect said yes or no, I don`t stop. I kept asking them to put me in front of new people.

The more I practiced doing this, the better I got. The better I got, the higher the odds were of new sign-ups putting me in front of their people. The better I got, the higher the odds were that those new people would say yes to joining our business. Again none of this is easy, but nothing worthwhile is. It takes time and dedication but I know this. Help the newest person right away by taprooting! If your new sign-up doesn`t put you in front of new people within the first 48 hours of signing up, their odds of ever doing anything greatly diminish.

My mentor taught me that people often don`t ask for referrals or learn the skill of taprooting because they don`t want to be seen as takers. It`s like the vampire swooping in and sucking the blood out of all the people. When he told me this, at first, it made sense to me, and I had this short-lived fear that all my friends would see me as a networking vampire. But my mindset shifted quickly. When I was in network marketing, my job was to help people with a product or help them with a business. My goal was to help the newest person quickly succeed with products and business. Anything I could do to help them with that was a win for both of us. Asking to meet with all of their best contacts was the best way to help them find success and train them on how to do what I was doing successfully.

When you help people find success quickly, they have much higher odds of sticking with it. So if you are in the same mindset, I was in, and are worried about being a networking vampire, remember that taprooting is a way to help the newest person find success quickly.

One of the biggest misconceptions about taprooting is that you can have huge success and coast into management mode because other people are recruiting. That is wrong! Don`t get stuck thinking that taprooting is management mode. It`s not. It is an active, engaging skill you can use in conjunction with the other skills I am teaching you. People don't misinterpret taprooting as a management mode where you can just be working with the same person. If that same person isn't putting you in front of many brand-new people, you need to reach out to new people personally. Remember working in this business is talking to new people about your products or business. You have to ask for the invite into a circle of influence and then get to work. You do this because that circle of influence may have been out of reach for you before you recruited this one person. The goal of taprooting is to get what you can.

I want to give you specific steps to start you off taprooting and knowing how to use this skill to SMASH your goals and get you to where you want to be in your network marketing business. First, I want you to start out thinking about one person. Who is the best person you know that you would feel comfortable presenting the business to? That is the person that I want you to get in front of your mentor or on a three-way call/chat, zoom, or messenger. Too many people are consuming and not going out and creating the business they want. Remember, urgency is synonymous with wealth, so I don't want you to wait on this and say, "I'm just soaking this all in! I can do this later." Put this book down, or stop the audible. Go and contact that person right now because this tool doesn't work unless you work the tool.

Ok, so once this person has signed up, we want to get them into action FAST. We aren't going to sit down with them and make the plan to start the plan. People are most excited right when they sign up. Don't wait three days or a week to get them going. Start the minute they sign up. Odds are they will be less likely to take action if you allow too much time. The very second, yes second, they sign up; I want you to ask them, "Who are the best people you know that come to your mind who you think would be fantastic at this business?" You can do the same for products and change your script to focus on the products.

You wait for their response. If they say, they can`t think of anyone, you prompt them to look at their contact list and break down everyone they know into four categories: friends, family, business, and community (community could be social media contacts). Every single person that they know will fit into one of these categories. This helps this person get into small action, and you can help them by encouraging them and reinforcing the action they are taking. Here is the best part: they haven`t had to do anything "scary" yet! For several reasons, it can be intimidating for people to give you contact names. Still, we want to start rewarding the action and showing people that doing this business is about small actionable steps. Be willing to walk them through their fears and hesitations with them. I find that the two biggest questions people have are, "Can I do it?" and "Is it worth it?"

Once they have their list, get them to send messages or texts to people. They can say something like, "Hey, what`s your schedule like tomorrow?" That`s it! It is that easy. Then you have them message them back when they start to get responses with something like, "Nothing, what`s up?" They can send a message saying, "Do you have a couple of minutes that we can chat? I want to share something with you that has just come up that I am excited about." Don`t get caught up in words. *The Ultimate Script Book* will explain that in more detail.

Once they get people saying yes, they simply share their stories. Remember the two questions everybody asks themselves? "Can I do this," and "is it worth it?" Show them how simple it is. All they have to do is share their story. Once they share their story, they turn it over to you, and you then plug them into whatever system your company uses. That`s it. Taprooting sounds complex, but it is the most underutilized, simple system out there.

Every company uses different types of systems, so I`m not going to go into detail about what to say next, but understand that taprooting is simply enrolling one person and then getting them to introduce you to their network. The key principle I want you to take away is getting your new people to immediately reach out to THEIR contacts. Mind drama gets in the way quickly when sharing about a new business opportunity or a product you have started to use. You have to help your newest person combat that drama by getting into action quickly.

An example I give is watching little kids learn to ride a bike. One of my son`s friends and he were learning to ride their bikes at the same time. One of them was willing to get into action quickly. He fell several times, but he was determined to keep trying. He was riding his bike around the neighborhood by the end of the day. The other boy had lots of fears and kept getting into his head. "What if the bike falls?" "What if I can`t stop?" "What if I stop too fast?" The questions kept coming, and he never got on his bike. He sat and watched his friend all day. Want to guess how long it took that boy to ride his bike? ALL SUMMER! The crazy part is that he spent the entire summer in fear and never once tried to ride. It wasn`t until he faced his fears and got into action that he realized that he would figure out what to do only when he was in action and trying.

The same thing applies to starting someone in their network marketing business. You can`t walk someone through all of the objections before they happen for them to finally feel good enough to take action and never have failure. Failure is part of growth. But we want it to be an actionable failure. Actionable failure means that we are taking action WHILE learning! Failing forward is key.

Taprooting is also about vision. You have to give them the right vision to see how getting their business going and sharing it will help them succeed. Maybe they told you they`re excited because of the humanitarian trips this money could provide. Maybe it`s taking their family on that trip to Disneyland. Maybe it`s just traveling the world or getting out of debt. Whatever their vision is, empower them and remind them why they`re excited to share their story.

I love to meet them where they are, and they usually start out pretty scared to make that first contact. I tell them, "I know you`re scared right now, but it`s not going to be any less scary a week from now. I`m going to help you, and let`s get you into action right now. Let`s contact your best five people.

When I started network marketing, there was no social media presence. Building your business was taboo to do anything on social media. This was over 15 years ago. So, I became the top recruiter of a million distributors by taprooting. I didn`t have social media to make contacts. There is an art to getting into someone else`s circle of influence, and it can be used repeatedly to create HUGE success, whether on or offline. Now, I`m not saying you shouldn`t be using social media. You absolutely should. Once I added social media, it only enhanced all of the principles I am teaching you. But you also need to use taprooting to never run out of leads.

There is an acceleration of trust that happens with taprooting that doesn`t happen online, and it makes a huge difference. Once people introduce you to their circle of influence and share your credibility with them, you will see how your closing ratio is much higher because there is some personal connection. Remember, at the beginning of this section, we talked about warm leads. Your taprooting leads will warm up a lot quicker than your online leads. But you have to get great at asking for FAST connections.

Simple Duplication

"It's hard to beat a person who never gives up."

— Babe Ruth

When the company Apple started, its first marketing brochure stated, "Simplicity is the ultimate sophistication." Steve Jobs, one of the founders of Apple, was known for his relentless pursuit to simplify things and eliminate unnecessary components of Apple's products. He was also known for doing that same thing in his personal life. Steve Jobs picked one outfit he would wear every day to work because it took out the need to think or take time trying to decide what to wear. Job said, "It takes a lot of hard work to make something simple, to truly understand the underlying challenges and come up with elegant solutions."

This example of Steve Jobs is crucial in our business. Let me explain. Let's say that you have invited people over to your house to learn more about the product that you are selling. You want to make a great impression on everyone. You spend hours cleaning your house, making gift bags for everyone, and even hiring someone to cater the event. You are focused on spoiling everyone during the event and going all out. You think you are doing it right and everyone will have a great time. They might, but you haven't created a duplicatable system for most people there that night. No one seems interested when you stand up and tell people about the opportunity to start their own business like you. You may be wondering what's up. The food was amazing, everyone gushed about their gift bags, and several people bought products. In your pursuit to make a successful over the top event, you may have created an unattainable expectation for those that attended. When you mention the business, people think, "I could never afford to cater an event." OR "I don`t have a house that looks like this." In your effort to impress, you forgot all about duplication.

Anytime you show up for your team, business, or social media, remember that you have eyes watching you. People are looking at what you do and how you do it, thinking if they can do the same thing. How are you showing them through THEIR launch how easy this is? If you make it out of reach for most people, you will detract people from the business opportunity.

As you launch people into their business, you have to keep it simple. You may think, "but Rob, I LOVE to spoil people, and I have a knack for parties and events." Don`t worry! There will be a time and place for all of that. But when someone is launching is not the time. Think about the newest person launching and all of the actions you want them to take. Walk through that process and ask yourself, could a junior high kid do this? If the answer is no, then you need to simplify the system.

Too often, we complicate our launch system to impress people. We want them to see the business and think how epic it is. Just like Steve Jobs said, there is sophistication in simplicity. Look through your launch system. Is it simple? Why do you do what you do in the launch? If you can`t explain each step simply, you may want to ditch it.

One of my clients heard me say that everything during a launch should be simple enough for a junior high kid. She went home that night and enlisted her son, who was in eighth grade, to go through her launch process. She later told me, "It was such an eye opener for me to have my son go through the system. He was confused about some parts, and the next step didn`t make sense. Looking back at my numbers, I realized that my new team members had told me the same thing for a year! Many of them would get stuck in that same spot. Instead of simplifying it for them, I quickly brushed it aside and had them move on." It wasn`t until her son walked through the system that she saw the need to simplify several areas of her launch process. Happy to report that her updated simple team launch system was so successful that it is now used company-wide.

I ran an entire boot camp all around duplication. You can find it on my podcast *Network Marketing Breakthroughs* starting on episode 61. I had different guest speakers come on and talk about their best duplication strategies and what works for them. Here are a few things that stood out to me in those conversations.

First, duplication is really about communication. If you can`t communicate the objective, expectations, and education, you will fail your newest person! Start with the objective when you meet with your person or walk them through something. Before social media, we were all about third-party validation through phone calls. That has changed! Now, most people are doing third-party validation through zoom meetings OR three-way chats on platforms like messenger, Wechat, etc. It doesn`t matter how you choose to do your third-party validation. Make sure you are using the principles that work!

The first principle of any third-party validation is the introduction. You must teach people how to introduce and validate who you are to the prospect. This is important because the prospect probably won`t know who you are. The prospect trusts their friend, so it`s essential to learn how to start the conversation by having your recruit introduce you.

Notice that the objective here isn`t to have your newest recruit close a deal; the objective is simply to learn how to introduce and validate.

The second principle of third-party validation is setting expectations with your recruit. You want them to know what success for them would look like through this process. You can say, "I expect you to be on the call the entire time. I expect you to start by saying hello to the person and introducing the person and me to each other. I expect you will give me 2-3 sentences about this person to help me get to know them, and then I expect you to validate me. I can take it from there."

This is the simplest way to help out the newest person. Set the objective and the expectation, and then educate them. Once we have had the three-way conversation, I will follow up with the person and give them quick feedback. "Great job today. I loved how you shared about the person`s hobby and why they were interested in the product. One thing that I would love for you to do next time is to say something like, "I`m going to let Rob take over from here because I know he has some great info to share."

Notice that I give praise. Make sure your praise is sincere. If they messed up most of the conversation, don`t lie to them and tell them they did great. Find something to praise. Then give them quick swift feedback. I always say swift because I want you to remember that you don`t want to overwhelm them. Instead of spending ten minutes telling them everything they did wrong, find up to two places they can improve.

Duplication is all about showing people how to be successful in this business. Network marketing is not hard. It is a simple business that has proven successful results for decades. Don`t try to sell people on this business by overcomplicating it. More and more people are looking for something simple. We are all busy with everyday tasks and challenges. No one has the time or energy for something complicated. Don`t kid yourself by thinking it looks more appealing to have the twenty-step process when it could have been done in two steps.

SKILL #6 CHALLENGE

One of the most simple and effective things is a 48 hr challenge. Pick a day and for the next forty eight hours, you are going to reach out to thirty people about anything that is non-business related. This can be making new connections or reconnecting with people. Have real conversations with people! It can be reaching out for anniversaries, birthdays, etc. More conversations done right make a huge impact.

After you do this, the next twenty four hours are going to be spent reaching out to twenty people to take a look at the business. You aren't trying to sell products or sell the business, you are selling them on taking a look!

SKILL #7 BUILDING A THRIVING CULTURE

> *"No matter how brilliant your mind or strategy, if you're playing a solo game, you'll always lose out to a team."*
>
> — *Reid Hoffman*

The culture of YOU (Branding)

> *"Your brand is what people say about you when you are NOT in the room"*
>
> — *Jeff Bezos*

When I think of building the culture of you, one person comes to my mind instantly; Gary Vaynerchuk, also known as Gary Vee Gary Vee started building his personal brand on Twitter with his perfectly timed responses and posts. He was unapologetically himself. When Gary Vee came onto the scene, this huge narrative was being pushed about what a good video was supposed to be like. Everyone was preaching how the professional video was the only way to go and how you had to be the polished version of yourself to get a reach and make an impact. There was also a massive push for how much you could show up on social media without overexposure in the market. Gary Vee wasn't buying into any of it. He decided to build a brand around himself and his personality. He is bold and decided to be raw and candid with his videos and interactions with people. Gary didn't care about overexposure and would post all of the time on every platform he could. He gained a loyal following quickly and expanded his brand by being himself. Gary has multiple income streams because of who he is and it has created an empire around him.

Gary is an example of why your personal brand means so much. He hasn't lost who he is based on the companies he has built or the outside products and services he is advertising. Your personal brand is your calling card to the world. It is how people know who you are, your values, and what you stand for. It is what draws and detracts people. Your personal brand can help build the know, like, and trust factor more than anything else. He helps people see what and who they are getting from their very first engagement with him.

I love using Gary Vee as an example because the man and his brand can be very polarizing for people. You either love or hate Gary Vee I think there is no higher compliment to knowing your personal brand than having polarizing opinions of you.

I love reading the comments I get on Amazon about my books. One night I was reading the comments on a book that had just been released. There was one that said, "Absolute waste of time. All this book is about selling and recruiting your face off." I read it to my wife with a grin on my face. She asked me why I was so pleased about that comment. I told her because there was nothing more complimentary than having a polarizing opinion of the book. I knew that book would be a huge success and help many people, and it has.

As you build your personal brand, I want you to consider what sets you apart from others. What values do you have that you live by? In what way do you love to interact with people? What passions and hobbies could you spend hours talking to others about? How do the people closest to you describe you? All of this is going to play into your personal brand.

Don`t lie to yourself and say that you don`t have anything interesting to say. Don`t shortchange yourself and NOT figure out your personal brand. This will be a huge mistake that will slow down your success. I walked one of my masterminds attendees through a personal branding exercise, and I could tell one woman was half-heartedly doing it. I called her out. "Hey, what`s coming up for you? I can tell you aren`t taking this seriously."

She said, "I know who I am. I don`t think it will be the type of person other people want to work with." I asked her what she meant. She then told me that she is loud, has a foul mouth, and loves to spend her weekends at the lake floating with a cold beer in her hand, loud country music, and off-color jokes. She said, "That`s not what a successful business person does. I like me, but I don`t see how that personal brand gets me anywhere in the business."

Here is what we all need to know. YOU, the real YOU, is precisely what is going to be attractive to your audience. If I had told this woman to tone down her language or not to mention what she likes to do on the weekends on social media, she would have failed. Instead, I told her to own her brand. I told her to go all in on the country music lake scene. I told her to connect and be herself.

She was surprised by my answer and said, "I never thought straight-laced Rob Sperry would be signing off on my colorful language!" She got to work creating her personal brand and has had HUGE success! Colorful language and all!! HA! That`s because it is authentic to her. Your personal brand is about letting people get to know you. It`s about showing up as yourself and being an example to people that are attracted to you. Don`t change who you are because you think that it is what will help you sell. Your authentic you is what will help people connect more profoundly with you.

One of the questions I get is, "Do I have to write down my personal brand?" The answer is I recommend it. It can only help. You have to know exactly who you are and what you stand for. When you write down your brand, I recommend you post it somewhere where you will see it. We all get lost sometimes in watching and seeing other people all of the time. We can lose ourselves quickly if we start the compare and despair game. You must be reminded of who you are and what you stand for. Look at your personal brand daily.

Growing up, whenever any of us kids would act up, my dad would ask us, "Are you just trying to get attention?" It became a negative thing to try and get attention. When I first started in this industry, I was pretty scared about branding myself because I still saw it as a negative thing and like branding yourself was trying to get attention. When I learned about this concept, it felt like it went against everything I was taught growing up. Branding you, really is just having people get to know you and who you are. I had to start diving really deep into this concept because it was a big obstacle for me. Give yourself permission to be your authentic self.

I finally started to see branding myself the right way and made a commitment to myself that I would never see personal branding in a negative light again. This helped me stay consistent on social media and start to get a following of people that were liking my content.

I once had a client come to me with this same block. They said, "Rob, I really hate having the attention on me. I don`t think I want to create a ME brand." Because I had already worked on this myself, coaching this person was really fun for me because I had done the work and I could help this person get over it too. I asked this person, "Who are big influential people in your life?" This person mentioned Ghandi and Jesus Christ.

I told them that both of those individuals got a lot of attention! Attention is the number one currency in network marketing. I always say that attention with the right INTENTION is how you can impact the world. All of the great people in the world had major attention with the right intention. Branding is going to help you set the right intention in your business and life!

The US brand (company culture)

"The most powerful enduring brands are built from the heart."

— Howard Schultz

Think about logos. When I say "swoosh," what comes to mind? For 98% of us, we thought about Nike. Nike is one of the most recognized brands worldwide. When I was traveling overseas last year, I was sitting next to a man on the plane who didn`t speak English and I didn`t speak Arabic. We smiled at each other as he sat down. He looked down at my shoes and said, "Nike," then gave me a big smile and a thumbs up. Nike is the world`s largest athletic apparel company known for its iconic shoes. It is a multinational brand, meaning that Nike operates worldwide. Many network marketing companies are multinational as well.

Nike has done a fantastic job at branding its company. From their well-known "Swoosh" logo to their commitment to sports and athletes. One of the things that stands out most to me about Nike as a company is its ability to have so many different athletes represent their brand while still staying within the culture and brand they have created.

Serena Williams was the queen of the court. She has had one of the most epic careers in all of tennis. She is one of the women who has brought high fashion to the tennis court in a way that no one ever has. One of the ways that she has done this is with her partnership with Nike. In one of her last professional matches at the US Open, Serena wore Nike shoes that had 400 hand-placed diamonds embedded in them. She also wore a design that Nike created that took inspiration from the figure skating world. It was a glittering long-sleeved dress with a skirt with six layers, one for each of her US Open titles. Watching her walk onto the court was such an inspiration to me. I knew the exact brand she was wearing because Nike stayed true to its brand. They did an excellent job showcasing Serena and her brand as well. It was the best example I have seen in years of what it looks like for a company and a person to collaborate ideally with their brands. I also went to New York with my wife and two older kids to watch her last tournament. It was crazy to see the brand she and Nike have both created. Both would succeed without each other, but together they are so powerful.

That is what you want to do with your company! You must work on branding yourself and seeing how your brand works with the company you represent. The US brand is created when a persona and the company are so in sync that you can see the person and company represented in their collaboration.

That is what you do with whatever network marketing company you have joined. You are collaborating with them to bring their products and your opportunity to as many people as possible. So what does it look like to create a US brand?

First, you have got to get to know your company. Who are they? How did they start? Is the owner still running the company? Who is the C-level team? How did the company get started? Where are they located? What is their mission and vision? You should always know the basic information about whatever company you are a part of. You can`t create the US if you don`t know what half of the partnership looks like.

Next, start to see how your brand fits with the company. How do you compliment each other? Why did you decide to go with this company? What is it about being part of the company that excites you? What are you most proud of about this company? As you answer these questions, I want you to start to see all of the reasons WHY you are creating an US brand. It will be challenging to create a rock-solid relationship if you are dating someone and are embarrassed to be seen with them. The same goes for creating a US brand with your company. If you haven`t already, start to fall in love with your company!

Finally, be realistic. Too often, we start with a company with rose-colored glasses. Just like any other relationship! Remember that people are running your company. People mess up, make mistakes, and maybe even hurt your feelings. My wife loved watching the show "This is Us." Like millions of people, she loved watching the relationships in the Pearson family, especially the BIG three, evolve and grow. If you have watched the show, you know that none of the characters are perfect. Every single person has flaws, screw-ups, and things that happen. It didn`t mean that they couldn`t have strong relationships with each other. As you look at your company, realize that mistakes will be made. Maybe your back office crashes on the last day of the month. Your best product may be out of stock for a while. It happens! One thing that keeps an US brand solid is seeing all sides of what is happening.

The US brand is vital because, like Serena Williams and Nike, everyone wins when the US brand is done correctly. Nike reported skyrocketing sales after Serena revealed her look on the court. The same week she played in the US Open, she had her line of shoe launch on Nike, and they sold out within seven minutes. Both Nike and Serena were winning. When you can infuse the US brand into your own, you will see significant shifts in engagement with others. Knowing the company brand so well shows how you present and offer your prospects. It also helps with the following brand we are going to be talking about; the WE brand.

The WE brand (your team)

"Don't wait until you are big to start building your brand. Build a brand from scratch alongside your business."

— Richard Branson

The WE brand is about creating a culture and is vital in your network marketing business. It is one of the most important aspects of becoming a better leader, and depending on your leadership level and the number of team members you have, you can still challenge yourself to start creating the WE brand that you want to be a part of. Remember that it doesn't matter how big your team is. You can start small. Like Stephen Covey says, "You need to begin with the end in mind."

The WE brand is about what type of team brand you are intentionally creating. This is everything from team names, how you communicate together, how you party, and what drives your team. I cringe whenever I hear the newest person say, "I don't think I will have to think about branding my team for a long time! It's just my best friend and me right now on my team." STOP. This is so backward and frustrating when I hear anyone say something similar to this for several reasons.

First, it lacks vision because you don`t see yourself having a team to lead. Second, it leads to a culture and a brand that isn`t thought out for a team. Think about a pregnant woman who doesn`t do anything to prepare because the baby isn`t here yet. And I`m not talking just about getting baby supplies. What happens if the mom doesn`t eat properly, goes to her appointments, and maybe even parties too hard? It has an impact on her baby. Have a vision of the future. When my wife and I were dating, I talked several times about having children. I envisioned my future and what I wanted it to look like. I knew I wanted to marry someone who wanted children as I did. My vision and her vision matched up, and we could frequently talk about it.

The WE brand will be created organically if you aren`t intentional about it. This can be fine, but I have also seen it go wrong really fast. For example, I had a guy come to me that had never heard of team culture or the WE brand. As I explained it to him, he nodded his head. He let out a big sigh when I explained it and said, "Yep, that`s my problem. I never created a team culture on purpose. I have some guys on my team that are cocky and overly competitive. It has created this crazy dynamic on team calls to the point where I don`t even want to show up anymore." It`s never too late to create a WE brand; it may take some time to adjust if you have a larger team.

The vast majority of people inside of network marketing are paying to be part of a community. We all have different communities that we invest our time, money, and energy to be a part of. Maybe it`s a sports team, a hobby, or a church. We all have that need to belong. And in network marketing, This is truly the business behind the business. If you want to create a next-level type of business, you need to challenge yourself on what type of WE brand you will want to create.

Think about what type of groups you love to show up in. Think about the dynamic that lights you up and also helps create safety for you. The guy I was talking to wasn`t feeling great about showing up to team training because of the dynamic that a couple of guys had infused into the team. The WE brand not only says what we want in a group but can also specify what we don`t want. Never be afraid to set boundaries in a community. That helps people feel safe and know that your group isn`t in the wild West where anything goes.

The WE brand is about starting a culture aligned with your vision and brand. It is the ultimate pinnacle of putting all of the brands together. It infuses the YOU and US brand and leaves room for others. I love seeing teams that have created the WE brand from the beginning. I have a couple that I work with who told me how they started network marketing with the vision to have 20,000 people on their team. They brainstormed for a week and came up with a community mission statement, the values they wanted their team members to live by, and a vision of what running a team that size would look like. Everything they did, came through the WE brand. They have stayed true to it, and I believe it is one of the things that draws people into their organization. It is truly incredible to see the power of the WE brand.

When I had a network marketing team, one of the things that were important to me was service. One of the things I did with my teams was create a random act of kindness day. We called it RAK, and it was like a random act of kindness blitz. We did simple things throughout the day. It could be like paying for someone`s gas, complimenting a stranger, helping with yard work, etc. It was fantastic to do as a team because people got so creative. I learned so many different ways to serve others.

This created the WE brand and culture I loved being a part of. Creating your team brand can be based on anything you want. You can create a brand that incorporates the fun factor through your posts or activities online or in person. You want to make people feel good about themselves and love to be a part of the community, so think about what will help you create that type of team brand.

Part of your WE brand is going to be recognition. I would challenge you to consider how many ways you can recognize based on effort. I spoke about this earlier. As much as celebrating rank advancement is incredible, you also have to celebrate the action taken. Some examples could be spotlighting someone once a week, celebrating birthdays, or shoutouts for someone supportive of others in the group. Celebrations will be a considerable part of your WE brand statement, so make sure you figure out and address what you want that to look like.

To create a WE brand, I want you to start with what you already know. What are your values? What helps you feel lit up about being in a group? What do you need in place to feel safe in a group? How do you like to celebrate in groups? What is the vision for the group? What is one thing you would love to do with your team members? How do you encourage people in groups? How do you give hard news to people in a group? If you can answer these questions, you are well on your way to creating the WE brand you will love to support, encourage, and be a part of.

SKILL #7 CHALLENGE

Write out the YOU brand. Who are you? What do you love? What do you want to be known for? Write out the US brand. What type of culture do you want to create? What is your team going to be known for? What helps your team stay connected and united? Write out the WE brand. How does your company work together with the YOU and US brand? How are you helping the company? What works well with all of it?

"The best revenge is massive success."

-Frank Sinatra

CONCLUSION

I love and hate this quote all at the same time. In many ways, it is an excellent motivator, but eventually you will outgrow revenge as your success because it is bigger than that. Every single person craves success. We all want to be successful. We want to be successful in our relationships. We want to be successful in challenges and tests. We want to be successful in business and with money. Let me share a story about a man who was sent to prison. He was ashamed of his actions and felt like a colossal failure. One day while he was feeling sorry for himself and sticking to himself in the library, an older inmate approached him and said, "If you keep looking like that, things will never change for you."

The ashamed inmate didn`t feel like talking, but what the older man said bothered him. "What do you mean things will never change?" He said, bothered that the old man had spoken to him. "I`m here doing the same thing every single day. Things won`t change for me for another seven to ten years."

The old man said, "Your address may not change for a bit, but everything else can."

The inmate waved the old man off and kept staring at the same page in his book he had been looking at for the past twenty minutes. When he returned to his cell, he couldn`t stop thinking about what the old man had said.

He couldn`t change what he had done to land him in prison. He couldn`t change what people thought of him. How could everything but where he lived change?

The next day he found the old man and asked him, "How can I change everything?"

The old man told him, "You can change everything by starting to succeed in every area of your life. Success isn`t just for the man in the business suit on Wall Street. Success is for EVERY man, woman, and child."

That struck the inmate hard. He realized that he hadn`t been succeeding before he came to prison, and he certainly wasn`t succeeding really at anything in prison. He wasn`t trying to improve himself or his situation. He sulked around and tried to keep his head down and stay out of people`s way.

After that, the inmate started to look for areas in his life where he could succeed. He found that even though his cell was bare and small, there were still ways he could improve it. He started to take making his bed more seriously. He tucked in the corners and straightened up the best that he could. He also ensured his clothes looked nice and would spit shine his shoes every morning.

When he started to make his own space and clothes nicer, he started to feel better. He decided he would start working out more intently, and even though he didn`t get a say in what he was eating, he could decide how he thought about the food and what he decided to eat.

The smallest changes started to add up, and the inmate started to see that what the old man said was true. Success could be attained by anyone, even an inmate in prison.

Most people think that success is this huge secret that only the super wealthy know and that they keep locked up away from everyone else. Success is for everyone. Everyone can look at their life right now and decide what to be successful at. Success is doing things with intention every single day. Success starts with the simple action steps you intentionally take every day. Consistency and time add up, and you will find that you can be one of the most successful people on this planet. I believe this intensely, and I live by the belief myself.

Success is for you. Success is action. Consistency combined with desire and vision fuel that success. This book has been about creating success in your network marketing business. I am passionate about helping people win in network marketing, and I have made it my life`s purpose. But I care deeply about personal wins and winning the silent battles we all face at one time or another.

We all struggle. Some of us struggle with things that others can see. Some of our struggles are so deep and personal that not even our spouses or loved ones know about them. Our struggles do not have to stand in the way of our success. We are meant to struggle. As I mentioned in this book, the struggle makes success so much sweeter.

I want you to know that you can be successful. I want you to picture it clearly in your mind. I want you to see that your success will align with your pure desires and vision for yourself. This means that your success is going to be unique to you. It is possible for you! You can make it happen.

In this book, I have done a lot of educating. We have gone through the seven skills everyone in network marketing needs to master to succeed. Now I want to give you some challenges that you can go through to start taking action in each of these steps. I suggest you follow the challenges in order as they will build off of one another. Once you have gone through them in order, you can use these challenges to help you grow in whatever area you see you need a boost. Each challenge will lead to different results and lessons you can learn as you work in each area.

BONUS Challenge DOING THE BASICS BETTER

For the next 60 days, create a daily method of operation that you will stick to. Write it down and hold yourself accountable. If you miss a day, you start over on day one.

- 1 New Post or FB Live

- 5 New Reach Outs (A reach out is a non-business message. It could be a new contact, or it could be an old friend. It is simply staying connected with others).

- 1 New ASK (Directly asking someone to look at your products or business)

- 5 New Friend Adds (Adding five new friends on social media)

- 1 Follow-Up

- At least ten pages of personal development

Lightning Source UK Ltd.
Milton Keynes UK
UKHW021339270123
416064UK00015B/1070